Ea... in Brazil

This book was provided for

WITHDRAWN

by

Bettendorf
Public Library
Foundation

Raising money to support,
enhance and preserve
Bettendorf Public Library
programs and services.

Eat Smart in *Brazil*

How to Decipher the Menu
Know the Market Foods
&
Embark on a Tasting Adventure

Joan Peterson

Illustrated by S. V. Medaris

GINKGO PRESS, INC

Madison, Wisconsin

Eat Smart in Brazil
Joan B. Peterson
© 2006 Ginkgo Press, Inc. All rights reserved. First Edition 1995. Reprinted 1996 and 1998.

Although the author and publisher have exhaustively researched all sources to ensure the accuracy and completeness of the information contained in this book, we assume no responsibility for errors, inaccuracies, omissions or any inconsistency herein. Any slights of people or organizations are unintentional.

Map lettering is by Gail L. Carlson; photographs are by Martha Laboissiere, Paulo Laboissiere, Tim Walsh, Joan Peterson and Susan Chwae.

The quote by James A. Michener from "This Great Big Wonderful World," from the March 1956 issue of Travel-Holiday Magazine, © 1956 by James A. Michener, is reprinted by permission of William Morris Agency, LLC on behalf of the author.

Publisher's Cataloging in Publication
(Provided by Quality Books Inc.)
Peterson, Joan (Joan B.)
    Eat smart in Brazil : how to decipher the menu, know
the market foods & embark on a tasting adventure / Joan
Peterson ; illustrated by S.V. Medaris. -- 2nd ed.
    p. cm.
    Includes bibliographical references and index.
    LCCN 2006922640
    ISBN-13: 978-0-9641168-9-4
    ISBN-10: 0-9641168-9-8

    1. Cookery, Brazilian. 2. Diet--Brazil. 3. Food
habits--Brazil. 4. Cookery--Brazil. 5. Brazil--
Guidebooks. 6. Brazil--Description and travel.
I. Title.

    TX716.B6P48 2006   641.5981
                                  QBI06-600086
Printed in the United States of America

To Deise and Martha

Their love and knowledge of Brazilian food

added savor to every page

Contents

The Cuisine of Brazil   1

An historical survey of the development of a unique cuisine influenced primarily by the cooking traditions of the native Indians, the Portuguese and the African slaves.

Regional Brazilian Food   13

A quick tour through the five regions of Brazil to see the extraordinary diversity of cooking styles encountered in traveling the length and breadth of this enormous country.

Tastes of Brazil   39

A selection of delicious, easy-to-prepare regional and national recipes to try before leaving home.

Shopping in Brazil's Food Markets   57

Tips to increase your savvy in the exciting outdoor food markets and modern supermarkets.

Resources   61

A listing of markets carrying hard-to-find Brazilian foods and of some groups that focus on travel to Brazil or offer the opportunity to have person-to-person contact through home visits to gain a deeper understanding of the country, including its cuisine.

Helpful Phrases   65

Questions in Portuguese, with English translations, which will assist you in finding, ordering and buying foods or ingredients, particularly regional specialties.

Menu Guide   71

An extensive listing of menu entries in Portuguese, with English translations, to make ordering food an easy and immediately rewarding experience.

Foods and Flavors Guide   99

A comprehensive glossary of ingredients and cooking methods in Portuguese, with English translations, including more-detailed descriptions of the unfamiliar foods to allow quick identification in the marketplace.

Preface

> If you reject the food, ignore the customs, fear the
> religion and avoid the people, you might better
> stay home. You are like a pebble thrown into water;
> you become wet on the surface but you are never
> a part of the water.
>
> —JAMES A. MICHENER

As an inveterate traveler, I have had many adventures around the world. I have traveled independently, relying on my own research and resources. One way I gauge the success of my trips is how well I become familiar with the native cuisine. To me, there is no more satisfying way to become immersed in a new culture than to mingle with the local people in the places where they enjoy good food and conversation, in their favorite neighborhood cafés, restaurants, picnic spots or outdoor markets. I try to capture the essence of a country through its food, and seek out unfamiliar ingredients and preparations that provide scrumptious new tastes. By meandering on foot or navigating on local buses, I have discovered serendipitously many memorable eating establishments away from more heavily trafficked tourist areas. As an unexpected but cherished diner, I have had the pleasure of seeing my efforts in learning the cuisine appreciated by the people in ways at make an understanding of each other's language unimportant.

Each trip energizes me as though it were my first; the preparation for a visit becomes almost as exciting as the trip itself. Once I determine the destination, I begin to accumulate information—buying most, if not all, the current, relevant guide books, raiding the libraries and sifting through my hefty collection of travel articles and clippings for useful data. A high priority for me is the creation of a reference list of the foods, with translations, from the gathered resource materials. For all but a handful of popular European destinations, however, the amount of information devoted to food is limited. General travel guides and phrase books contain only an overview of the cuisine because they cover so many other subjects of interest to travelers. Not surprisingly, the reference lists I have compiled from these sources have been incomplete; many items on menus were unrecognizable. Of course, some menus have translations but these often are more amusing than helpful, and many waiters cannot provide further assistance in interpreting them. Furthermore, small neighborhood establishments—some of my favorite dining spots—frequently lack printed menus and, instead, post their daily offerings, typically in the native language, on chalkboards outside the door. So unless you are adequately familiar with the language of food, you may pass up good tasting experiences!

To make dining a more satisfying cultural experience for myself and for others, I resolved on an earlier trip to improve upon the reference lists I always compiled and research the food "on the spot" throughout my next trip. Upon my return, I would generate a more comprehensive guide, making it easier for future travelers to know the cuisine. The book that resulted from that "next trip" featured the cuisine of Brazil and represented the first in what became a series of in-depth explorations of the foods of foreign countries. To date seven other EAT SMART guides have been published. These explore the cuisines of Turkey, Indonesia, Mexico, Poland, Morocco, India and Peru. The guides for Turkey and now Brazil are in their second editions. My intention is to enable the traveler to decipher the menu with confidence and shop or browse in the supermarkets and in the fascinating, lively outdoor food and spice markets with greater knowledge. A number of the vegetables and many of the extraordinary tropical fruits in Brazil appear nowhere else but in these outdoor markets.

Everyone confesses both to disliking certain foods and to avoiding others that are unfamiliar. This guide will help steer the traveler away from known problematic foods and will encourage sampling new and unusual ones. The informed traveler will have less concern about mistakenly ordering undesirable food and will, as a result, be more open to experimentation.

My own journeys have been greatly enhanced because I have sampled unfamiliar foods. One of many illustrations of this in Brazil is my experience on a boat trip out of Manaus on the Amazon River. I was introduced to the unique flavors of some of the myriad tropical fruits and to preparations of exotic local fish such as the enormous *pirarucú*, whose flesh resembles the white meat of chicken more than that of fish. These remarkable yet simple feasts were created by the boatman's wife in a crude, lean-to kitchen off the back of the boat. Later, I was taken by canoe through the flooded forest to densely overgrown, upland fruit orchards, and saw growing there some of the same fruits I had just tasted—delicious fruits I would find again in the outdoor markets and in restaurants as key ingredients in tortes, ice creams, jams, jellies, even wines. These orchards belonged to *caboclos*, the inhabitants of the Amazon interior, who offered me samples of still more fruits, which I savored during my unforgettable nighttime return to port. Sitting on the boat's rooftop deck, I was entertained by a spectacular display of firefly pyrotechnics and the stars of the southern skies, unobscured by the pollution of civilization.

This guide has four main chapters. The first contains a history of Brazilian cuisine. It is followed by a chapter with descriptions of regional Brazilian food. The other main chapters are extensive listings, placed near the end of the book for easy reference. The first is an alphabetical compilation of menu entries including typical Brazilian fare as well as specialties characteristic of each of the five regions of Brazil: the north, northeast, center-west, southeast and south. Outside a particular geographical area, these specialties rarely are available unless a restaurant features one or more regional cuisines. The classic regional dishes that should not be missed are labeled "regional classic" in the margin next to the menu entry. Some noteworthy dishes popular throughout the country—also not to be missed—are labeled "national favorite." The second list contains a translation of food items and terms associated with preparing and serving food. This glossary will be useful in interpreting the menu since it is impractical to cover all the flavors or combinations possible for certain dishes. Descriptions of the unfamiliar yet glorious tropical fruits are more detailed to make it easier to recognize them in the fruit stalls of the open-air markets and city sidewalks. Likewise, the characteristics of the indigenous fish are described for those who venture into the fishmarkets (a must) and then encounter the same fish on menus.

Also included in the book is a chapter offering hints on browsing and shopping in the food markets and one with phrases that will be useful in restaurants and food markets to learn more about the foods of Brazil. A chapter is devoted to classic Brazilian recipes. You are encouraged to take time to experiment with these recipes before departure as a wonderful and immediately rewarding way to preview Brazilian food. Most special Brazilian ingredients in these recipes can be obtained in the United States; substitutions for unavailable ingredients are given. Sources for hard-to-find Brazilian ingredients can be found in the chapter containing resources. This chapter also cites some groups that offer the opportunity to have person-to-person contact through home visits to gain a deeper understanding of the country, including its cuisine.

I call your attention to the form at the end of the book. I would like to hear from you, my readers, about your culinary experiences in Brazil. Your comments and suggestions will be helpful for future editions of this book. This form can also be used to order additional copies of this book and other EAT SMART guides directly from Ginkgo Press, Inc.

Boa viajem e bom apetite!

JOAN PETERSON
Madison, Wisconsin

Acknowledgments

I gratefully acknowledge those who assisted me in preparing this book. LouAnn Englebert for translations; Martha Laboissiere, Deise Dutra, June Parreiras, Corália Medeiros, Leticia Anand, Circe Zugno, Jane Ambrosio, Anisia Quirino da Silva, Fatima Silverio and Emilia Martins Mateus for contributing recipes from their private collections; Marvin and Ellouise Beatty, Janet Beatty, Deise Dutra, Circe Zugno, Martha Laboissiere, June Parreiras, Leticia Anand and Roberto Narimatsu for help in identifying menu items and regional foods; S.V. Medaris for her magical illustrations; Martha and Paulo Laboissiere for splendid photography; Gail Carlson for enlivening the maps with her handwriting; Susan Chwae for a knockout cover design and author photograph, and Nicol Knappen of Ekeby for bringing the text neatly to order.

I am indebted to John Lyons (Wisconsin Department of Natural Resources), Peter Bailey (Illinois Natural History Survey), Michael Goulding (Amazon Rivers Project) and the late Lynn Messinger for help in identifying the amazing fish of the Amazon; Nigel Smith and Hugh Popenoe (University of Florida) for helpful discussions on the extraordinary fruits of Brazil; Paul Bosland (New Mexico State University) for background on the popular hot *malagueta* peppers; John Schuon, Jim Escalante and Adam Steinberg (University of Wisconsin) for useful information about typography and printing, and Thomas Yuill (University of Wisconsin) for directing me to key resource people.

Thanks also to Kevin Clark, Martha Laboissiere, Brook Soltvedt and Erin Dickerson for taste-testing the recipes; Klindt Vielbig and Norman and Audrey Stahl, whose unofficial newspaper clipping services kept me well supplied with timely articles about Brazil; Marvin and Ellouise Beatty and Archibald Haller (University of Wisconsin) and A.F. and Winnie Bartsch

ACKNOWLEDGMENTS

(Pan-American Health Organization) for their instructive reminiscences of Brazilian cuisine; and Patricia Werner for her unflagging encouragement.

I gratefully acknowledge Francisco Pereira, Martha Almeida, Valdir Coelho and Maria do Socorro, members of the Servas organization in Brazil, for introducing me to several scrumptious Brazilian dishes in their homes or favorite restaurants.

And special thanks to Brook Soltvedt, a most perceptive and helpful editor.

Eat Smart in **Brazil**

Guyana
Venezuela
Surinam
French Guiana
Colombia
Ecuador
Brazil
Peru
Bolivia
Chile
Paraguay
Argentina
Uraguay

South America

The Cuisine of Brazil

An Historical Survey

The extraordinary cuisine of Brazil is an amalgam of the cooking heritage of three disparate groups of people: the native Indians, the conquering Portuguese and the African slaves they brought to work in the sugar cane fields. The cuisine did not evolve, however, by absorbing these influences, eliminating their identities in the process. The distinct contribution of each of these cultures is still apparent in many Brazilian dishes today. Interestingly, the national cuisine of Brazil is more a collection of unique regional cuisines.

Of course, certain dishes underwent transformation and in the process took on a new "Brazilian" identity. The Portuguese added their own stamp to several Indian preparations and, in turn, the Africans altered some of the dishes of both the Indians and the Portuguese. They used foods and cooking styles brought from their homelands or brought their own recipes and changed them, taking advantage of local ingredients. It was the African cooks in the plantation kitchens of the sugar cane barons, however, who in colonial times developed many of the dishes that are now-famous in the northeastern region, and provided the strongest influence in generating what would be considered a Brazilian cuisine.

European immigrants—Germans, Italians and Poles—as well as Japanese and other groups, came in huge numbers much later. Many farmed the extreme southern region of Brazil or worked the coffee plantations, and they brought their own traditions of cookery and delicious dishes, adding to the growing Brazilian culinary repertoire. These homesteaders, however, had little lasting impact on the Brazilian style of cooking. Their cuisines retained their own identities rather than becoming a part of the native, Portuguese and African cooking traditions that are recognized today as Brazilian cuisine.

1

The Indians

The coastal Tupi Indians were the first aboriginal people to interact with the Portuguese when they arrived in the New World in the early 1500s. They taught the early colonists how to adapt to their new environment, how to use the many unusual foods growing there, and how to cultivate these crops.

The main staple of these natives was the manioc tuber, a carbohydrate-rich food that is easy to propagate but difficult to process, at least for the bitter variety, which is poisonous when raw. It is astonishing that the Indians determined that these tubers were edible at all. To detoxify manioc, the tubers had to be peeled and grated and the pulp put into long, supple cylinders—called *tipitis*—made of woven plant fibers. Each tube was then hung with a heavy weight at the bottom, which compressed the pulp and expressed the poisonous juice. The pulp could then be removed, washed and roasted, rendering it safe to eat. The product was a coarse meal or flour known as *farinha de mandioca,* which is as basic to the diet of Brazilians today as it was to the early Indians. Starch settling out from the extracted juice was heated on a flat surface, causing individual starch grains to pop open and clump together into small, round granules called tapioca. The extracted juice, boiled down to remove the poison, was used as the basis of the sauce known as *tucupí.* In the northern region of modern Brazil, several noted and delicious dishes incorporate this traditional sauce.

Manioc meal became many things in the hands of the Indian women. For the children, small, sun-dried cakes called *carimã* were prepared. There were a porridge or paste known as *mingau,* and thin, crisp snacks called *beijús,* made of either tapioca flour or dough from a sweet, non-poisonous variety of manioc known as *macaxeira* or *aipim.* Pulverized manioc meal was mixed with ground fish to produce a concoction called *paçoka,* or *paçoca* as it is known today.

TIPITIS

2

The humid, tropical environment of the northeast was unsuitable for wheat and several other crops the Portuguese colonists depended on. They were forced to develop many new eating habits based on indigenous foods. Out of necessity they quickly learned from the native Brazilians how to make manioc meal and prepare some dishes from it to sustain them in the New World. The Indians introduced them to the non-poisonous tubers of sweet manioc, which are somewhat fibrous but considerably easier to prepare; they are pared, boiled for several hours to soften them and eaten like potatoes. Corn was another Indian foodstuff that the colonists used as a substitute for wheat. Like the Indians, the Portuguese made porridges of corn called *acanijic,* which can be found today as *canjica* or *mugunzá,* and used corn husks as containers to steam a sweet mixture of corn and coconut called *pamuna,* which came to be known as *pamonha.*

Other important food crops grown by the Indians were yams, sweet potatoes, squash, beans, peppers, peanuts, pineapples and gourds. Vegetable greens, however, never had a significant presence in the indigenous diet. To this day the diet of many Brazilians includes few leafy green vegetables. Certain native fruits, such as the *cajú* (cashew apple), papaya and guava, appear to have been semicultivated and an extensive variety of other fruits were easily gathered from the wild. Indians also propagated bananas. The caffeine-rich seeds of the fruit called *guaraná* were made into a beverage, valued both as a stimulant and for its putative aphrodisiac powers.

Fish were plentiful. What the Indians did not consume immediately they salted and dried. As important then as now, the mammoth *pirarucú* fish provided much-needed protein in the highly starchy Indian diet. Fish was generally prepared simply by boiling or roasting it over coals, although a more elaborate procedure involved wrapping the fish in banana leaves prior to roasting. This dish the Indians called *pokeka* and it subsequently inspired the African version called *moqueca,* a stew with fish or shellfish, flavored with coconut milk, hot pepper and the palm oil known as *dendê.*

The Portuguese augmented the basic Indian methods for cooking fish, adding their expertise in fish preservation to the local cuisine in the form of *bacalhau.* This beloved dried saltcod is still an important commodity imported to Brazil today and a common menu item with countless means of preparation.

The Indians also obtained protein from the manatee, which they called *peixe-boi,* or cowfish, because its snout resembled that of a cow, and from the turtle. A preserve called *mixira* was made from manatee meat by roasting it in its own oil and then sealing the pieces in earthenware jars, a process that was applied to fish and game as well. Turtle meat and eggs were especially delectable food items and a stew called *paxicá* was prepared from the turtle liver. Both species are endangered today, but are nevertheless prized as foods.

The lasting contribution of the native Indian to Brazilian cookery is especially evident in June on the joyous midwinter festival days, called *Festas Juninas,* when the feasts of St. John, St. Anthony and St. Peter are celebrated throughout Brazil with traditional foods, games and dance. While these customs originated with the Portuguese, the origin of many of the dishes associated with these holidays in Brazil is unmistakably native. Prominent among the customary culinary preparations are baked sweet potatoes and the indigenous corn-based dishes of *canjica,* or *mugunzá,* and *pamonha.*

The Portuguese

The coast of Brazil was already a legal Portuguese possession before Pedro Álvares Cabral discovered it in 1500—by chance according to some accounts, having been blown off course on a voyage originally intended for India. The rights to this land were made possible by the Treaty of Tordesillas, signed by Portugal and Spain in 1494, which effectively parceled the lands of the New World between them. Portugal was entitled to lands east of a meridian some 370 leagues to the west of the Cape Verde Islands and Spain was entitled to those west of it.

The first Portuguese to arrive in Brazil, at what is now the city of Porto Seguro in southern Bahia, were essentially traders, who saw little other than the plentiful dyewood called *pau brasil* that might be profitably traded in the New World. For the next several decades, occasional forays were made inland by these brazilwood merchants, or *brasileiros,* to obtain this commodity for which the new land ultimately was named. Their efforts supplied the European textile industry with a fashionable bright red dye from the pigment that bled from the wood.

It was not until the 1530s that settlers arrived. The Portuguese Crown divided the land into *sesmarias,* vast parallel tracts of land, each 50 leagues wide with no apparent boundaries inland, and gave them with hereditary rights to minor nobility in exchange for undertaking colonization. In 1549 the first governor, Tomé de Sousa, was sent to rule Brazil from Salvador da Bahia do Todos os Santos, or simply Salvador da Bahia, the new capital.

Boi, or bull, the central figure in the *bumba-meu-boi* folk drama, which is enacted on the midwinter festival days every June.

Of the early colonies, only the one at Pernambuco in the northeast was particularly successful.

Realizing that the soil and climate were ideal for sugar cane growth, the colonists brought plants from the Azores and began cultivating a narrow strip of land along the coast between the present-day cities of Recife in Pernambuco and Salvador da Bahia in Bahia. Since sugar was precious to the Europeans, indispensable for medicinal purposes and highly prized as a foodstuff, the plantation owners anticipated their venture would be very profitable. The colonists intended that the Indians, either voluntarily or enslaved, would work the sugar cane fields, but this arrangement did not succeed for a variety of reasons, and the plantation owners—at least the wealthier ones—began to turn to Africa for slaves instead. This was to have a profound effect on the country and on its cuisine.

By the middle of the sixteenth century when the slaves began arriving, the diet of the Portuguese was already heavily dependent upon native foods such as manioc, corn and fish. They actually had come to appreciate the indigenous foodstuffs that they had originally eaten out of necessity because the climate did not allow for wheat production. Portuguese traders even introduced to the African continent both manioc and the Indian way of processing it into an edible form. The preference for manioc and corn flours over wheat is apparent in many areas of Brazil today. A great variety of these flours is available, including the fine, sweet or sour types, called *polvilhos,* made from tapioca starch. Cheese rolls called *pão de queijo* made from *polvilho* flour and eaten while still warm are incomparable.

Initially, the plantation pantries were not well stocked with good food. Few could afford imported Portuguese foods such as cheese, olives, dried fish and fruit or even wheat flour, which were shipped to the colony infrequently and often were rotten or unnutritious by the time they arrived from Portugal. Good meat and fresh vegetables were rare. So important had sugar cane production become in the coastal regions that other food crops were not cultivated and domestic animals were not raised for meat, for fear the animals would destroy the cane. A better diet prevailed in the south, where the growth of sugar cane was only moderately successful, and the early settlers planted other food crops.

In marked contrast, the nuns who came to Brazil set up gardens in their convents and raised a variety of domestic animals and fowl; their food was abundant and nutritious. In this new setting, the nuns continued their tradition of making preserves, sweets and confections, using copious amounts of egg yolks and Brazilian sugar. Their products were sold in local markets and exported to Europe, where sugar was scarce. This fondness for rich, sometimes excessively sweet desserts was inherited from the Moors who had occupied Portugal for many centuries. Also surviving the transition to Brazil were the popular names given to these confections—names such as "angel's cheeks," "Mother Benta," and "maiden's drool,"—which are still used for these popular treats throughout Brazil today.

Eventually, food products brought from the homeland did expand the national menu. These included cheese made from sheep's milk, saltcod, olives, olive oil, and almonds. The Brazilian cuisine became enriched with Portuguese dishes such as the delicious stews called *cozidos* and mixtures called *frigideiras* containing meat or fish, especially saltcod, baked with beaten eggs— dishes that would be embellished further when the Africans came. The Portuguese introduced the process of cooking with wine, especially Port and Madeira, and a method of preserving meat by drying. Appetizers or *salgadinhos,* literally meaning "little salties," such as savory pies *(empadas)* and turnovers *(pasteis),* developed into a national passion and became even more varied with the incorporation of native ingredients. Made larger, these *salgadinhos* became scrumptious main dishes.

A characteristic modern Brazilian cooking style, contributed by the Portuguese, uses either of two preliminary processes to enhance the taste of meat, fish or seafood. The "*refogado*" technique calls for lightly sautéeing these ingredients in onion or garlic (or both), with tomatoes and seasonings in a little oil to seal in the succulent flavors. The other technique entails marinating the food in a "*vinha d'alho*," a mixture of lemon juice or vinegar with crushed garlic and seasonings, to flavor and tenderize it. Meat, fish and seafood pretreated in this Brazilian manner are undeniably flavorful. It is incredible that a recent guide book says that Brazilians do not do very much with meat, other than just cooking it!

The Africans

The Brazilian kitchen already showed many signs of dual culinary heritage when the Portuguese plantation owners began to import slave laborers from Africa to toil in their sugar cane fields in the middle of the sixteenth century. The bondage of these black Africans was to last for 350 years. The cooking style they brought to Bahia added a dimension that would define a truly Brazilian cuisine. This second and more significant transformation of the cuisine had to wait, however, until the masters no longer determined what dishes the slaves assigned to cook in the "big houses," or *casas grandes,* of the plantation were allowed to prepare. Once the slave cooks gained control of the menu, they were able to make their own traditional dishes for the extended plantation family, improvise upon them and upon the established fare, and in the process create dishes with a more Brazilian identity.

African cookery had an unmistakable character that added an entirely new taste to Brazilian cuisine. Its main ingredients were hot *malagueta* peppers, the thick milk squeezed from freshly grated coconut and the bright red-orange oil from the *dendê* palm nut. Dishes typically were heavily laced with pungent, ground shrimp that had been dried and smoked, peanuts or cashews and a variety of spices, such as ginger, fresh coriander and cumin. Okra was introduced as both a vegetable and as a thickening agent.

Much of the African food set on colonial tables had the consistency of soft, porridge-like mashes or purées. Among these preparations were *vatapá, acarajé, carurú, bobó,* and *abará. Vatapá* became the most famous dish, typifying the essence of Afro-Bahian cooking. It is a thick purée of dried shrimp, cashews, peanuts, bread and coconut milk, colored a vivid yellow or orange-yellow by the inclusion of *dendê* oil and given added zest with onion, garlic, ginger and *malagueta* peppers. *Vatapá* also serves as a filling for the appetizer known as *acarajé,* a fritter made from a batter of dried, ground shrimp and ground beans. The skins of the beans are laboriously removed beforehand, following an overnight soaking. Dollops of batter, fried and flavored in sizzling dendê oil, are slit open and stuffed with a bit of *vatapá.* A special sauce for these bean cakes, *molho de acarajé,* contains *malagueta* peppers and dried shrimp, and is also used as a filling.

Several meat and fish dishes eaten today were also prepared by the African cooks. *Xinxim de galinha* is a delicious stew with large pieces of chicken in a sauce of dried shrimp, nuts, seasonings and *dendê* oil. Coarsely chopped beef and sliced okra are the basis for the dish called *picandinho de quiabo,* or *quiabada. Efo* features fish with a type of steamed red spinach leaves known as *lingua de vaca,* or cow's tongue, flavored with coconut milk, dried shrimp and *dendê* oil.

The African slaves modified existing dishes from the menus of their masters to suit their own tastes. To the baked saltcod dish *frigideira* they added coconut milk, replaced the fish with cashew nuts and substituted *dendê* oil for the olive oil favored by the Portuguese. *Moquecas,* delicious fish or seafood stews with the characteristically African components of coconut milk and *dendê* oil, were derived from the *pokeka* of the Indian, a simpler preparation of fish and peppers roasted over coals in a bundle of banana leaves. In the African version, the banana leaves were eventually replaced by a black clay cooking vessel. Thick and savory molded cornmeal mushes, or *angús,* reminiscent of Indian corn porridges, accompanied main dishes. The fluffy *farofa,* another side dish, was elevated from the ordinary by browning the plain manioc meal in butter or oil and adding an assortment of flavorful ingredients.

Cooks who were exceptionally talented at preparing the special Afro-Bahian dishes were highly regarded. Many famous literary and musical figures immortalized these notable artisans in poetry and song, calling them *quituteiras* because they were especially adept at creating tidbits, or *quitutes,* as they are called in Portuguese.

Although the African dishes underwent modification over time in the plantation kitchens and assumed a more Brazilian identity, they remained basically unchanged in the *terreiros,* or religious houses, where food was an integral part of the religious rites. The slaves came from many African nations and had diverse religious backgrounds. Most became nominally Catholic, but in a practice known as syncretism, continued to worship their own gods by enveloping their identities in safe Catholic counterparts to avoid persecution. The tribal religion of *Candomblé* practiced by the West African slaves was to play a key role in preserving the African cuisine because it mandated that the ritual food offered to the gods follow precise recipes. Central to *Candomblé* was worship of ancient deities called *orixás,* who have specific tastes requiring particular preparations of food. Each *orixá* has a consecrated color, specific garments, a favorite food, and a special day of the month on which to be worshiped in the sacred *Candomblé* house, or *terreiro.* The complex ritual of cooking was considered holy. On the designated day of celebration, the *orixá's* special food was elaborately prepared, using traditional recipes and cooking methods so the god would not reject the food because its taste had changed. An offering of the meal was then placed at the *orixá's* shrine. A similar presentation was also made to the *orixá* named *Exu,* who is the intermediary between the deities and their worshipers, although some identify him with the devil. He has the power to keep things under control or create havoc, and no one wanted trouble during the ceremony that followed. *Exu* had a fondness for *cachaça,* the heady brandy made from sugar cane, and he always was given some of this.

There were numerous African specialties to accommodate the appetites of the many different deities. *Oxalá,* god of creation, was the most important. His symbolic color was white, so white foods, such as white corn, were offered. The god of fire and lightning, *Xangô,* and one of his three wives, *Yansã,* the goddess of the winds and tempests, preferred *dendê* oil and *malagueta* peppers because red was their color. Fittingly, *Yansã's* ritual food was *acarajé,* bean and shrimp cakes fried to a rich orange-red color in *dendê* oil. *Oxum,* the second wife of *Oxalá,* was the goddess of fountains and beauty. Her color was yellow, as was her special food, *xinxim,* a spicy chicken stew flavored with *dendê* oil. *Oxala's* third wife, *Yemanjé,* goddess of waters and mother of all the *orixás,* favored fish. *Ogun,* god of iron, was fed *feijoada,* a hearty stew taking up to a full day to prepare. It contained black beans, smoked sausages, dried beef and variety meats, such as pigs' feet, tails, ears, and tongues. This epicurean spectacle, once unworthy of the plantation masters, has become the national dish of Brazil.

The Immigrants

Portugal relinquished sovereignty over Brazil in 1822, providing the opportunity for enormous numbers of immigrants from Europe, Asia and the Middle East to settle in the relatively unoccupied land in the south or work the expanding coffee plantations on the São Paulo plateau. This assured Brazil an ample labor force when the slaves were emancipated in 1888. By 1930, over 4 million people had come.

To encourage this migration to Brazil, the government offered incentives such as free ocean passage and financial aid to help farmers get established. Land-hungry immigrants came from many nations. Germans began to arrive in 1824, settling primarily in the extreme southern region of the country in the states of Rio Grande do Sul and Santa Catarina, where both the terrain and temperate climate were reminiscent of home. A small contingent of Italians came in the 1850s, followed by more extensive migration beginning in the 1870s. Many also established homesteads in Rio Grande do Sul and Santa Catarina. A group of Swiss immigrants, arriving a few years before Brazil became independent, settled in the state of Rio de Janeiro. Poles and Russians set up colonies in the state of Paraná. Considerable numbers came from Spain, and later, from Japan and the Middle East. Even the Portuguese were represented in the mass migration to Brazil—this time as foreigners. The European colonists transplanted to Brazil their agricultural system of diversified farming, cultivating many different crops on a single farm and raising livestock for both meat and dairy products. In Rio Grande do Sul the Italians developed a robust wine industry.

By 1860, coffee had became the beverage of choice for most Brazilians, replacing long-established drinks such as *garapa,* the juice extracted from sugar cane, or *aluá,* a fermented concoction made from sweetened corn meal and water. Coffee was grown on large, labor-intensive plantations, or *fazendas,* in the state of São Paulo, using a system of slavery similar to that of the sugar cane plantations in the northeast. It was clear, however, that the institution of slavery was not going to drive the wheels of coffee production much longer. After 1850, it had become unlawful to import slaves. Many of the slaves had already been freed when, in 1888, slavery was officially abolished. Savoring their freedom, the emancipated slaves left the plantations in droves to begin a new life with a whole new set of rules in the cities. Immigrants replaced the freed slaves on the coffee plantations, signing on as wage earners or sharecroppers until they were able to acquire land of their own. Others chose to earn a living in the city of São Paulo.

With the arrival of numerous ethnic groups, the Brazilian menu expanded to include many new and delicious international entries. The Italians introduced rich, cheesy pastas made from noodles and these joined rice as popular side dishes accompanying main meals. They brought *risotos* and their version of corn porridge, called *polenta,* a dish quite similar to the African *angú.* The Germans contributed many items, including sauerkraut, spaetzle and liverwurst, and since they had successfully cultivated the potato in their adopted country, potato dishes also appeared on the menu. Although previous attempts to cultivate wheat in the southern region of Brazil had not been wholly successful, Italians and Germans in the late 1800s had better results. Both groups grew wheat, enabling them to make some of their native European foodstuffs. Settlers from the Middle East offered their raw lamb and bulghar (cracked wheat) dish called *quibe* (kibbeh) and *tabule,* (tabouleh), the refreshing salad made of softened bulghar, minced green onions, parsley, and mint in a lemon juice and olive oil dressing. All groups enhanced the cuisine of Brazil with new dishes, but these foods mostly retained their ethnic character rather than becoming Brazilian.

THE NORTHERN REGION OF BRAZIL

Regional Brazilian Food

A Quick Tour through the Five Regions of Brazil

The North

The northern region of Brazil has seven states: Amazonas, Pará, Acre, Rondônia, Amapá, Roraima and Tocantins. Their combined area includes almost all of Brazil's large portion of the great Amazon River, its tributaries and the rain forest, collectively called Amazônia. This region contains the most diverse collection of species on earth.

In the early 1600s the Portuguese asserted their claim to the northern region of Brazil, expelling French, English and Dutch intruders who had set up small outposts in the region. Our Lady of Presépio Fort was established in 1616 at the site of the present-day city of Belém, strategically placed at the southern entrance of the Amazon river. The Portuguese also set up several forts in the Amazon basin, including one that is now the city of Manaus. By the middle of the eighteenth century there were about fifty settlements along the river banks. The north underwent little further development until the latter part of the nineteenth century when the rubber boom catapulted the cities of Manaus and Belém into great prosperity and importance. The euphoria was short-lived, however, because the success of plantation rubber in Malaysia, an industry started with smuggled Amazon rubber tree seeds, drove down rubber prices and ended Brazil's monopoly in 1912. Today, mining, manufacturing, lumbering and, in Manaus, free-trade zone status, sustain the economy. Many visitors to Manaus and Belém, still the area's two major population centers, spend a day or two exploring these historic and friendly cities before taking off on excursions on the river or into the rain forest.

RUBBER SEEDS

The Amazon basin was home to Tupi Indians, relatives of the same tribe of Indians who met the first Portuguese arrivals on the northeast coast. Their diet of manioc, corn, beans, yams, peanuts, peppers, wild fruits and fresh fish is still very much in evidence today among the inhabitants of the north. Much of the population lives in small settlements in houses built on stilts along the main rivers, or along the maze of narrow channels called *igarapés,* formed when the river floods and cuts through a region of the jungle. These inhabitants of the hinterlands, or *caboclos,* are of mixed Portuguese and Indian ancestry. For many, growing and laboriously detoxifying the poisonous variety of manioc grown on nearby land above the flood level is a way of life. The coarse meal produced from these tubers is a complement to every meal, sprinkled generously over just about anything.

The cuisine of the north draws heavily on its Indian heritage. One of the best-known dishes is *pato no tucupí,* duck marinated in lemon juice, oil and garlic, then roasted, and finally boiled in *tucupí,* a sauce made with the liquid extracted from grated manioc tubers and seasoned with *jambú* leaves and chicory. *Jambú* is an intriguing jungle plant whose leaves and stem produce a very faint numbing sensation in the lips and tongue. This herb is also an important component of a flavorful seasoned soup called *tacacá,* which contains dried shrimp and tapioca topped with *tucupí* sauce. It is traditionally served in bowls fashioned out of gourds, or *cuias.* The classic dish *maniçoba* is a stew containing various dried, smoked and fresh meats, along with giblets. It is flavored with ground manioc leaves, or *maniva,* which also color the stew a dark green.

Many dishes feature fish, a basic dietary component in the north. Some preparations use a spice called *urucu(m),* or *colorau,* as a flavoring and coloring. *Urucu(m)* is made by coarsely grinding the orange-red seeds from the berries of the annatto tree. The spice is known in the United States by the name annatto or achiote. *Caldeirada* is a popular fish stew similar to a bouillabaisse. The most valuable commercial fish of the region is the mammoth *pirarucú,* marketed primarily in a dried salted form. Its delicious flesh is quite meaty, almost like chicken. A popular dish made with this fish is *posta de pirarucú seco ao leite de côco,* or a slice of fish served in a delicious coconut sauce.

Certain inedible parts of this fish are also valued. The large, brown-tipped scales are sold as fingernail files and are used in a variety of handicrafts, especially masks. Even the tongue is recycled, its raspy surface useful as a grater. Another economically important fish featured on menus is the tasty *tambaquí*. This amazing fish is equipped with powerful, molar-like teeth for crushing its food—the fruits and seeds, especially the hard seeds of the rubber tree, that fall into the water of the flooded forest. A regional specialty is picadinho *de tambaquí,* which is a mixture of fish pieces served with rice, *jambú* leaves and toasted manioc meal. The beautifully colored *tucunaré,* or peacock bass, is also a prized food fish. It is the coveted catch of fly-fishermen who are beginning to discover the thrills of angling for it in the Amazon basin. A considerable number of catfish, such as *surubim, caparari* and *filhote,* can be sampled. *Filhote* are juvenile specimens of the largest fish of the Amazon, the giant *piraíba,* which reaches lengths of 10 feet and weights of 300 pounds. All of these fish must be tried in the restaurants and seen in the markets!

Some of the most traditional and best-loved dishes native to the Amazon region are made with turtle *(tartaruga)* and its eggs, and manatee *(peixe-boi).* Although these are endangered species and won't appear on the menu, some restaurants still offer them.

Perhaps Brazil's greatest treasure is her bounty of fruit. Many varieties of tropical fruit are not cultivated but grow freely in the wetland areas or in the uplands. Some are palm fruits. As is true for so many of the natural features

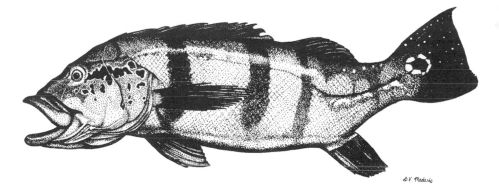

Tucunaré, the colorful and prized food fish of the north, has a distinctive mottled black patch behind the eye, 3 vertical blotches along the midline and an "eye" spot on the tail fin. It is one of the most desirable catches of adventurous fly-fishermen in the Amazon Basin.

of the land, most fruits bear Tupi Indian names. Even today some of these fruits are unknown in other regions of the country, particularly in the south. To the tourist the sheer variety of new and unusual types can be an overwhelming experience.

Brazilians use fruits in many ways. They are eaten raw, made into juices, jellies, marmalades, compotes, fermented beverages such as wines and liqueurs, syrups, flavorings for ice cream, desserts of endless combinations, and in many instances made into a sweet firm paste of fruit pulp mixed with sugar. The names for these pastes typically end with "*ada.*" For example, the fruit we know as guava is called *goiaba* by the Brazilians, and in the form of a sweet paste becomes *goiabada.*

In Manaus and especially Belém, the outdoor markets are a showcase for the regional fruits. The *Foods & Flavors Guide* in this book provides detailed descriptions of fruits and other produce to help with their indentification in the markets. To truly experience Brazil, try as many of these fruits as you can!

Among the palm fruits are *pupunha, acaí, buriti (miriti), patauá, bacaba, tucumã* and *uxí. Pupunha,* which has yellow, orange-red or green skin when ripe, is usually sold with the fruit still in clusters on the stems. It is never eaten raw. Rather, it is boiled and eaten warm, often with honey placed in the depression left by the large seed. The small, blue-black palm fruit called *acaí* is made into a juice that becomes a purple paste when manioc meal and sugar are added. The mixture tastes somewhat like black raspberries. Colorful cooking oils can be extracted from some of the palm fruits. *Buriti* generates a red oil, *patauá* a light-green oil, and *bacaba* a yellow one.

Some other fruits to look for are *cupuaçu, cacau, graviola, cajá, bacurí, cajá manga, jaca, murici, ata* or *fruta do conde, ingá, jambo, maracujá* and *biribá.* The aromatic *cupuaçu* is an easy favorite. This fairly large (up to 10 inches long), oblong fruit with a tough brown exterior and light-yellow pulp is closely related to *cacau,* whose seeds are the source of chocolate. *Cupuaçú* forms the basis of many popular desserts, including cakes, tortes and puddings. The sweet juice made from *cupuaçu* pulp becomes a delicious drink and is an ingredient in many desserts such as *torta do pará,* which specifically features the familiar Brazil nut called *castanha do pará,* native to the state of Pará. The *graviola* is a somewhat lopsided dark-green fruit with numerous soft spines on the surface. It makes a marvelous flavoring for ice creams, or *sorvetes.*

Two of the most exceptional fruits are *guaraná* and *cajú. Guaraná* is one of the best-loved fruits in Brazil and much folklore is based around it. The edible part is the black seed within some white, fleshy material. When ripe, the fruit has an uncanny resemblance to the human eye as it "peers" out of its opened, bright orange-red capsule. Ingesting the seeds produces high energy levels, which the Indians attributed to supernatural powers, but which we now know is the effect of caffeine. A legend of the Sataré-Maué Indians explains why the seeds resemble eyes. A beautiful Indian woman named *Onhiamuacabê* gave birth to a child sired by a mysterious being. This child was killed for eating some forbidden nuts, and at his burial site, a *guaraná* bush grew from his eye. According to the legend, the bush also brought forth a child from whom the Maué tribe descended. To the Indians, the seeds not only were a stimulant, they were an aphrodisiac and a means to prolong life. They roasted and ground the seeds, mixed them with manioc meal, and rolled the resulting paste into sticks, which were allowed to harden. Using the rough-surfaced tongue of the *pirarucú* fish as a grater, they broke off small pieces of the dried *guaraná* paste and rehydrated them in water to make a drink. *Guaraná* is available today in a variety of forms, including a very popular carbonated soft drink of the same name, a syrup, a powder, in capsules and in sticks made by the *caboclos*.

Guaraná, the fruit that resembles the human eye when ripe, has a large black seed within a fleshy white coat. The edible seed, rich in caffeine, is processed into a variety of beverages, including a carbonated soft drink of the same name.

THE NORTHEASTERN REGION OF BRAZIL

Cajú, or cashew apple, is a red or yellow fruit, resembling a bell pepper, with a pear-like taste. The cashew apple is not the real fruit, however, but the swollen flower stem. The true fruit is within the kidney-shaped sac dangling from it. Most unexpectedly, inside the sac, waiting to be roasted, is a cashew nut!

The Northeast

The northeast region of Brazil is comprised of nine states: Maranhão, Piauí, Ceará, Rio Grande do Norte, Paraíba, Pernambuco, Alagoas, Sergipe and Bahia. This part of Brazil consists of two quite different terrains: the vast semi-arid interior and the fertile coastal plains. The drought-stricken backlands of the northeast, the *sertão,* are characterized by subsistence farming and cattle and goat ranching on estates run by cowboys called *vaqueiros.* This is in marked contrast to the narrow strip of land along the northeast coast with its lush tropical vegetation and hundreds of miles of magnificent beaches. All of the states have ocean frontage with stretches of sand so fine as to be compared to walking on clouds. This area is emerging as Brazil's primary tourist destination. On the coast, where the sugar empire began and prospered by the sweat of slave labor, there is a vibrant African culture, centered in the city of Salvador da Bahia, where its influence is stronger than anywhere else in Brazil.

Beginning in the colonial era, some of the slaves imported from Africa served as cooks for the sugar barons in their grand mansions, and they dominated the plantation kitchens for most of the 350 years that slavery existed. A distinctive Brazilian cuisine evolved as these cooks improvised on many of their own traditional dishes and on those of the Indians and the Portuguese masters. At the heart of Afro-Brazilian (Afro-Bahian) cuisine are three ingredients that give a unique flavor and piquancy to the dishes: coconut milk, hot *malagueta* peppers and a palm oil called *dendê.* *Malagueta* peppers are considered so essential that a container of them, minced in oil, usually appears on tables along with salt and black pepper.

Travelers to Salvador da Bahia may have their first encounter with its famous cuisine as they stroll in the city streets. From *tabuleiros,* large trays or table tops set up along the sidewalks, black Bahian women sell both savory and sweet home-made tidbits. Their presence is announced by a whiff of the aromatic *dendê* oil simmering in large pots.

It is said that the history of the region resides in the food prepared by these picturesque Bahian women, or *Baianas*. In earlier times, as slaves, they brought to market a variety of treats on behalf of the plantation mistresses. Many ultimately were able to buy their freedom when they had accumulated enough money from their small portion of the profits. Today's *Baianas,* descendents of these proud women, offer the same tidbits and still wear the traditional white turbans, bouffant white skirts and lacy tunics, accented with many strands of beads and jangly bracelets.

On the trays of the *Baianas* are pans full of batter for bean fritters known as *acarajé* and pots of sputtering *dendê* cooking oil, the bright red-orange oil extracted from the nuts of a West African palm tree that was successfully transplanted to Brazil. This oil flavors and colors the fritter at the same time. Dried shrimp, pulverized with shells, is a traditional component of *acarajé* and many other dishes. Close at hand are bowls of the easily recognized bright yellow paste called *vatapá,* the most renowned of the many mashes or purées developed by the Africans, along with mounds of unshelled shrimp, fresh or dried, and other condiments and sauces for further embellishment of the bean cakes.

Traditional candies, cakes and puddings of many types can be found on the sweet trays. The African food tradition was not rich in desserts but the slaves in the *casas grandes* learned to make and then modify them, often by adding indigenous ingredients. Many recipes were obtained from the Portuguese nuns who brought to Brazil their knack of dessert cookery. Sweets were characterized by the lavish use of eggs and sugar, and coconut milk was often substituted for cow's milk. Representative confections include the irresistible egg and grated coconut upside-down dessert known as *quindim,* and cakes of manioc flour, eggs, cashews or peanuts, and brown sugar called *pe-de-moleque,* or "little boy's foot." Another version of *pe-de-moleque,* one that is more like a dark peanut brittle, is also available, as are patties of white or brown coconut candy known as *cocada,* neatly arranged in stacks. The dark version of *cocada* contains burned brown sugar. An interesting confection called *acaçá,* made of corn meal and rice flour and bundled in banana leaves, and a rich pudding of tapioca and coconut called *cuscuz de tapioca* also tempt the sweet tooth. This *cuscuz* (couscous) was a rather liberal adaptation of a non-sweet Moorish dish that probably came to Brazil with the slaves.

In the plantation kitchens, cake making developed into a competitive and rather secretive art. Recipes for super-rich, elaborate cakes were devised and

CAJÚ

given appealing, catchy names, often related to the plantation owner or historical events of the time. Thus there are cakes, or *bôlos,* named *bôlo cavalcanti* and *bôlo souza leão. Bôlo 13 de maio* commemorates the day the slaves were emancipated, May 13, 1988. Others have clever names like *bôlo espera marido* ("hoping for a husband" cake) and *bôlo quero mais* ("I want more" cake). These recipes were carefully guarded and passed on through the generations. Sometimes, when the recipes were written down, the master would deliberately exclude a key ingredient.

Afro-Bahian cuisine has four traditional sauces, or *molhos,* that accompany its special main dishes, and all include the indispensible hot *malagueta* pepper— actually a chili. Each sauce accompanies specific main dishes. The sauce known as *molho de acarajé* contains dried shrimp, cilantro and ginger and it complements the bean fritters called *acarajé,* and several famous dishes such as *carurú, efo* and *xinxim. Molho de pimenta e limão* is a pepper and lemon sauce served with *moquecas* and the glorious national dish of Brazil, *feijoada. Molho de azeite de dendê e vinagre* contains *dendê* oil and vinegar and it accents a codfish and coconut milk dish called *bacalhau com leite de côco* and a stew called *escaldado. Molho de nagô,* named for one of the African tribes brought to Brazil, contains pulverized dried shrimp and okra, and it accompanies stews such as *cozido.*

In Pelhourinho square in Salvador da Bahia there is a marvelous government-run restaurant school called SENAC *(Serviço de Educação Nacional de Artes Culinarias),* which offers an inexpensive, all-you-can-eat buffet containing a wide selection of the famous Afro-Bahian dishes. This sampler also includes a variety of desserts and it is the best introduction the traveler can have to the culinary heritage from Africa. The establishment sells a booklet of recipes made in the school; it may now be available in English as well as in Portuguese.

21

The role of African religion as an inspiration for cooking is especially evident in the city of Salvador da Bahia. Many of the dishes prepared by the slaves originated from the tradition of leaving offerings to their gods. This importance given to food can be witnessed by arranging with a travel office to visit any number of *terreiros* where the African rites of *Candomblé* are observed. Since the deities, or *orixás,* each have to be served a ritual meal that is prepared without deviation from the customary recipe, the continued presence of the famous dishes of the slaves appears assured. These foods for the gods are also delicious fare for the mortals!

Outside of Salvador da Bahia, there is less African influence in the cuisine. Plenty of fresh fish and seafood are available in the coastal regions and are featured menu entries. A type of crab called *aratú* is popular, as is *sururú,* a variety of clam. Seafood stews feature several combinations of lobster, squid, oysters, octopus, crab and shrimp. Some typical dishes are *siri mole,* soft-shelled crab cooked in a spicy sauce, *peixe na telha,* fish cooked and served on tiles, *agulhas fritas,* fried needlefish and *casquinho de carangueijo,* cooked crabmeat mixed with coconut milk, tomatoes and seasonings, returned to the shell and baked. A traditional Portuguese speciality is *dobradinha com feijão branco,* a tripe dish with white beans in a tomato-based sauce. Thin, crisp pancakes of fried tapioca with coconut, called *beijús or tapioca com côco,* make wonderful appetizers, as do breaded crab claws known as *unhas de carangueijo.* An interesting small green squash with a bumpy surface, known as *maxixi,* is made into a tasty stew called *maxixada* with dried meat, shrimp and tomatoes. *Pirão,* a soft mash usually of manioc meal, is a frequent side dish. A preparation called *arroz de cuxá,* found only in the state of Maranhão, is made with rice and vegetables seasoned with both the young leaves of *vinegreira,* or red sorrel, and its sesame-like seeds.

Exotic tropical fruits of all descriptions, many essentially unknown even in other parts of country, abound in the market place. To name just a few, there are *acerola, maracujá, pitanga, ata* or *fruta do conde, jaca, cajú, sapotí, graviola, pitomba, cupuaçu, cajá, jaboticaba, mangaba,* and *imbú (umbú).* A favorite is the *ata* or *fruta do conde.* Its delicious white pulp tastes somewhat like a pear. The *acerola,* a small, red fruit with three longitudinal furrows on its surface, makes a refreshing, tart juice with a cherry-like flavor and high vitamin C content. The most frequently encountered varieties of *maracujá,* the wrinkly passion fruit, are yellow, purple or red. Its many small seeds are surrounded by a delicious, juicy pulp, which can be scooped out with a spoon and strained from the seeds. The *pitanga,* another small red fruit, has deep longitudinal ribs on the surface. Try to taste them all! Most hotels offer sumptuous breakfasts that always include several different juice choices. In or out of season, thanks to the availability of frozen fruit pulp, juices and ice creams made from these fruits can be savored. The *Foods & Flavors Guide* in this book describes a great many of the fruits in detail to make their identification in the markets easier.

On the street, juice from sugar cane, *caldo de cana,* is squeezed on the spot, using an elaborate and often noisy metal contraption. Sugar cane from the northeast is famous for another popular drink derived from it, a brandy known as *cachaça*. It can be served straight for strong stomachs but more typically is blended with fresh fruit juice to make coolers known as *batidas*. When *cachaça* is combined with crushed lemon and sugar, it becomes the national drink, the *caipirinha*. The lemons in Brazil are small, green and tart— more like our limes. Street vendors also sell a delicious treat, called either *queijo de coalho* or *queijo assado,* made with a square of firm cheese that is barbecued and served on a skewer.

A totally different life style developed in the "other northeast" inland from the verdant and tropical coastal region of the northeastern states. By the 1600s, descendents of the Portuguese colonists, hardy people of mixed Indian and Portuguese heritage called caboclos, populated the harsh, semi-arid backlands. They established cattle ranches, or *estâncias,* to provide beef for the coastal region and became known as *vaqueiros,* Brazil's cowboys of the northeast.

The *ata*, or sugar apple, is a green fruit up to 4 inches long with many small bumps studding the surface. The segmented white pulp is sweet and delicious, tasting somewhat like a pear. Other names for this fruit are *pinha* and *fruta do conde.*

The *pitanga,* or Surinam cherry, is a red or dark-purple fruit about an inch in diameter with 7 or 8 longitudinal ribs. The orange-red pulp is delicious, sprinkled with sugar.

Their herds were derived from the cattle brought in 1549 to Bahia from Portugal by the first governor of Brazil, Tomé de Sousa. The soil was poor in the *sertão* and the animals had little to eat except the leaves from shrubs and trees. The people subsisted primarily on corn, beans and manioc, and sun-dried meat from their emaciated cattle.

The *sertão* is often inhospitable, as long periods of drought follow brief episodes of rain. After a rainfall, the moisture rapidly evaporates in the hot sun and the land dries out again. Not much grows except the desert-like *caatinga,* a type of sparse vegetation characterized by stunted trees, cactus and thorn-covered bushes. In periods of persistent drought, the coastal cities become inundated by masses of *sertanejos,* as the inhabitants of the *sertão* are called, looking for refuge.

The *vaqueiro* is unlike the *gaúcho,* the cattleman on the rich prairies of the southern region of Brazil. The northeastern cowboy tends to be somewhat downtrodden and resigned to the harsh life in the dry interior. His traditional clothes are made of sturdy leather to protect himself from the sharp thorns of the *caatinga* while tending the herds of cattle and goats. Once a year, in full leather regalia, the cattlemen gather together to celebrate a special outdoor *Missa do Vaqueiro,* or Cowboy's Mass, in the Pernambuco backlands in the city of Serrita, remaining on their horses during the ceremony. Included in the blessings are some that are specifically said for the cowboys' gear, their hats, saddles and saddlebags containing foods from the backlands that they brought to share. Typically this food includes manioc meal, *queijo do sertão,* a popular hard cheese made mostly of goat's milk, and *rapadura,* hard chunks of raw brown sugar eaten as candy.

Dried meat is an important foodstuff in the *sertão* and a common ingredient in the dishes of the region. *Paçoca* is a mixture of pounded, sun-dried meat and toasted manioc meal and, because it keeps well, it is a staple for the *vaqueiros*, who travel great distances rounding up stray cattle. Another typical dish is *baião de dois*, rice and beans with sun-dried meat in coconut milk and topped with melted goat cheese. *Cuscuz de fubá*, a mixture of chicken with corn meal and coconut, *buchada*, a tripe dish, and *bode assado*, roasted goat, are also identified with the area.

The northeast is rich in folklore. One of the most popular folk celebrations is the burlesque pantomime called *bumba-meu-boi*, or "hit my bull." Apparently originating as a pagan festival, it has become part of the repertoire of the winter festival days in June called *Festas Juninas*. Its performances are traced to colonial times when it served as a diversion for the slaves on the cattle estates. As is typical with folklore, the tale has many versions but the general theme is a satire pitting the black slave, or sometimes the lowly worker, against the oppressive master. The basic plot involves a slave, or a *vaqueiro*, who gets into some sort of mischief that causes the death or disfiguration of the master's prize bull and finishes joyfully with a miraculous resuscitation of the animal. It is enacted with many extravagantly dressed characters who sing and dance, musicians and a bull, the central character, made of a wooden frame covered with brightly colored cloth and exaggerated horns gaily decorated with ribbons.

Clay figurines depicting several characters in the popular *bumba-meu-boi* folk drama, considered the most interesting of the burlesque pantomimes of Brazilian folklore.

Mato Grosso
Goiás
Mato Grosso do Sul
Distrito Federal

THE CENTER-WEST REGION OF BRAZIL

THE CENTER-WEST

The states of Goiás, Mato Grosso and Mato Grosso do Sul make up the center-west region of Brazil. Much of the land is characterized as *cerrado*, a dry, savanna-like open prairie covered with patches of low scrub vegetation and twisted trees. To the north, the *cerrado* gives way to more wooded terrain. This region of the country contains the Pantanal, the habitat of an astonishing array of wildlife. It is a vast area of swamp and grazing land that periodically becomes flooded by heavy rains. The center-west is also the site of the ultramodern city of Brasília, inaugurated as the nation's new capital in 1960.

Exploration into this region was begun in the 1600s by adventurers called *bandeirantes* who undertook long expeditions deep into the interior of the country, searching for gold, diamonds and Indians to enslave for their own purposes or to sell to the sugar barons of the northeast. Their name was derived from the word for flag or banner, *bandeira*, since each group carried a standard that identified it. These rugged frontiersmen were mixed-race descendents of Indian women and Portuguese settlers from the vicinity of present-day São Paulo. They ranged as far as the Amazon in the north and even to the Andes in the west. During the long periods of migration, temporary villages were established in the backlands. Some of the *bandeirantes* remained behind at these villages and built remote colonies there. The discovery of gold and diamonds in the late eighteenth and early nineteenth centuries in present-day Goiás and Mato Grosso, and especially in Minas Gerais in the southeastern region, opened the area to further settlement. At the end of the gold boom, many stayed on in the mining towns and used the land for cattle grazing. Much of the prairie was divided up into huge estates called *fazendas* or *estâncias* and today, cattle ranching is a thriving industry. Agriculture became a mainstay as large crops of rice, corn, soybeans and manioc were produced. The building of the new capital out in the *cerrado* helped to open up the interior of the country but the region still is very sparsely populated.

Both meat and fish dominate the menu of the region. Since cattle are abundant, there is plenty of steak to be had. A wide selection of fish, some probably unfamiliar to the first-time visitor, tempts the palate. The *pintado*, a catfish, appears on menus in a popular dish called *pintado na telha*, or fish cooked and served on a tile. Other frequently served catfish are the *surubim* and *barbado*. Probably the most sought after quarry among fishermen is the

Minas Gerais
Espírito Santo
Rio de Janeiro
Rio de Janeiro
São Paulo
São Paulo

THE SOUTHEASTERN REGION OF BRAZIL

delicious *dourado,* which resembles salmon. The notorious *piranha* is featured in a regional soup called *sopa de piranha.* Silvery *pacús,* similar to but somewhat larger than the *piranha,* appear in a dish named *pacú assado com farofa de couve.* The fish is baked with a mixture of kale and manioc meal toasted in butter.

Special dishes made with pork are very common. *Pernil de porco,* a delicious roasted fresh ham, and *lombo de porco,* or roast pork loin, are examples. Some regional specialties feature chicken. *Frango à caçador,* or hunter's chicken, is a preparation made with chicken, potatoes, rice and vegetables. Several recipes feature the seed kernels or the granular pulp of the souari nut, or *pequí,* which is from a tree common to the *cerrado.* The classic dish *galinhada* has shredded chicken in a mixture of rice, corn and olives and is seasoned with *malagueta* pepper and a pinch of saffron. Adding the seed kernels of the *pequí* imparts a distinct flavor to the dish, which becomes *galinhada com pequí.* A popular side dish, *arroz com pequí,* adds the nut to rice, turning it yellow. Another rice dish, *arroz com guariroba,* uses a variety of bitter palm heart, sometimes called *palmito amargo,* which is derived from the *guariroba* palm.

Also representative of the area are some variations of the popular Brazilian tidbits called *bolinhos,* or small balls. *Bolinhas de arroz* are made with leftover rice; *bolinhas de queijo* are fried balls of a mixture of grated cheese and whipped egg white. Corn is a common component of sweets and snacks. *Pamonha* is a treat made from corn mixed with sugar, coconut and spices and steamed in corn husks. A similar concoction is called *curau.*

THE SOUTHEAST

The southeastern part of Brazil contains the states of Minas Gerais, Espírito Santo, Rio de Janeiro and São Paulo. This region is the industrial heart of the country and the location of Brazil's two major cities. São Paulo, the wealthiest state in the country, also has the largest city, the very cosmopolitan São Paulo visited for its dynamic, big-city atmosphere and fascinating night life. The state of Rio de Janeiro boasts its *cidade marvilhosa,* or marvelous city, the world famous Rio, set in one of the most dramatic and exquisite places on earth. Minas Gerais, or general mines, received its name in recognition of its great wealth of mineral deposits discovered during the late 1600s. It is especially renowned for its picturesque historic cities, now well-preserved national monuments, which came into existence during the gold rush of that time. The beautiful countryside of Espírito Santo with its many ranches and its coastal fishing villages is waiting to be discovered by tourists.

The present-day city of São Paulo came into existence in 1554 as a Jesuit mission on the site of an Indian village. This area became the point of departure for early explorations deep into the interior by *bandierantes,* the nomadic descendents of the Portuguese settlers and Indian women, who were more interested in scouting for precious metals and Indians to enslave than staying at home. The settlement remained small until the demand for coffee took hold some three hundred years later. The pressing need for a large labor force to work the nearby coffee plantations after the abolition of slavery led to a huge influx of foreigners, many of whom chose city life and made São Paulo a city of immigrants.

In São Paulo, as in the southern region of the country, where immigration also was extensive, ethnic enclaves maintain the traditional foods representative of the myriad nationalities that migrated to Brazil. Every imaginable type of cuisine can be found.

Few restaurants in São Paulo offer Brazilian cuisine perhaps because the *Paulistanos,* as the residents of the city are called, may prefer to savor this type of food at home. (Residents of the state are called *Paulistas.*) Two dishes are perhaps most representative of the area's contribution to Brazil's menu. *Camarões à paulista,* or shrimp in the *paulista* style, is a preparation of unshelled shrimp marinated in cilantro-seasoned lime juice and fried in olive oil and garlic until crispy. *Cuscuz paulista* is an elaborate dish that bears little resemblance to the couscous of North Africa. It is a mild and flavorful molded mixture of corn meal and manioc meal blended with sardines, palm hearts, sliced tomatoes and hard-boiled eggs, and olives. It is steamed in a special couscous pan called a *cuscuzeiro.* When unmolded onto a serving platter it is quite impressive.

Much of the food representative of the state of Minas Gerais reflects the mining era that was triggered by the discovery of the mineral lode in the highlands. Gold began to replace sugar as the country's economic base. The sugar industry was undergoing a gradual decline, facing stiff competition from foreign production in the West Indies, and many came to Minas believing that they had a better chance for success here. Found by the *bandeirantes,* gold, and later diamonds, attracted countless numbers of miners, including sugar planters and their retinue of slaves from the northeast.

Corn became an important food of the *bandeirantes.* It matured faster than manioc, which made it a more desirable crop for their nomadic life style. This food staple was adopted by the miners and settlers in Minas Gerais for their own consumption and it also doubled as feed for their mules. Various corn-based dishes eaten then are still present on today's menu. A molded corn porridge called *angú* or *angú de milho* is popular, as is its sweetened version, *canjica,* which is based on white hominy or grated fresh corn with coconut milk, condensed milk, peanuts and spices. *Pamonhas,* corn husks stuffed with a sweet corn and coconut mixture, are common.

Other representative foods are pork, black beans and leafy kale, or *couve.* A well-loved traditional dish in the style of Minas that contains these ingredients is *tutú à mineiro.* The word *tutú* refers to the bean component, which is mashed in this dish. *Couve à mineira* is shredded kale sautéed in oil, onion and garlic. *Feijão tropeiro,* or "mule driver's beans," contains whole black beans served with eggs, sausages, and pork chops. If the beans are puréed instead of being whole, the dish becomes *virado de feijão.* A variety of beans are popular throughout Brazil, but black beans are the favorite in Minas. Pork is featured in many other classic dishes, such as *lombo assado,* roast pork loin, and *leitão pururuca,* roast suckling pig basted with hot oil to make the skin crisp and bumpy. Cracklings of fried pork skin known as *torresmos* accompany most dishes. Especially addictive are delicious small rolls called *pão de queijo* made with fine tapioca flour and grated cheese, and a sweet caramel dessert called *doce de leite* made from thickened milk and sugar.

The settlement at the site of present-day Rio de Janeiro gained considerable importance during the gold rush era, when it served as the preeminent port from which the gold from Minas was sent to Europe. The economic center of the country shifted to the south, and in 1763 the nation's capital was moved from Salvador da Bahia to Rio, where it remained until the capital moved to the newly built city of Brasília in 1960.

The *Cariocas,* as the inhabitants of the city of Rio de Janeiro are known, are unabashedly passionate about their most typical dish which is also the national dish of Brazil, *feijoada completa.* It originated as a slave meal on the sugar plantations in Bahia and contains black beans and a variety of meats, especially pork. The requisite ears, tails and feet it contains were the undesirable parts of the pig that the masters declined to eat. This meal takes many hours to prepare and almost as much time to eat. *Cariocas* typically eat *feijoada* on Saturdays. Much of the day is devoted to partaking of this dish, starting at mid-day to allow time to recuperate afterwards. The meats and beans are simmered together for flavor and separated for serving. The tongue traditionally is placed in the center of the platter with the rest of the meats, such as sausages, salted and sun-dried beef, spareribs and the pork extremities, arranged around it. A special hot lemon and pepper sauce called *molho de pimenta e limão* is served with the meal. Other accompaniments traditionally served are sliced oranges, shredded kale, rice and manioc meal browned in butter. Diners often choose to begin the meal with some *cachaça,* the Brazilian sugar cane brandy, mixed with any number of juices to make a cooler called a *batida.* In the major hotels, the presentation of the meal is often somewhat different for the tourists. Individual meats are kept in separate pots, labeled as to their contents, and the diners select what they want to eat.

The popular *churrasco*, a grandiose barbecue, derives from an outdoor meal originating in Brazil's southern region and adopted by the *Cariocas* as their own. It features grilled meats of all kinds, and in certain restaurants it is served in the *rodizio* style—on skewers from which select pieces are chosen in an all-you-can-eat setting. A prized meat is *cupim,* the nicely marbled meat from the dorsal hump of the zebu steer. Brazilians have been known to walk out of a restaurant if this selection is not included.

Other popular dishes are *bife à cavala,* steak served with a fried egg on top, *rabada,* or oxtail stew, *bacalhoada,* saltcod with vegetables, *aipim frita,* or fried sweet manioc, and a preparation called *camarões casadinhos,* meaning "married shrimp"—two large shrimp, stuffed with manioc meal, placed side by side on a skewer and grilled. *Cozido,* a meat and vegetable stew, and *picadinho,* a chopped meat dish, are also typical menu items. Some excellent restaurants also feature regional food from the north and northeast.

The *Cariocas'* love for meat is shared by much of the country, so it is not surprising that an inordinate number of different cuts of meat are available. In 1980 the nomenclature was simplified, but many of the popular old names are still in general use, appearing on menus and at the meat markets. One of the most popular cuts of beef is a steak called *picanha,* which has a characteristic strip of fat running along one edge. Its name has an interesting origin. The meat is derived from a muscle in the rump region just in front of the tail. In the past, when oxen pulled carts, the animals were often encouraged to go faster by giving them a poke, or *picada,* with a stick in this area.

As cosmopolitan as Rio is, it still has large outdoor food markets. These lively markets are set up just a few blocks from the famous beaches and are fun to stroll through to become familiar with the varieties of fruits and vegetables popular in the region. Since they are held in several different locations and on several days of the week, it is easy to find one.

The small state of Espírito Santo is not frequently visited. Those who travel there can sample the *moqueca capixaba,* which is a seafood stew patterned after the Afro-Bahian *moquecas* of the northeast. It traditionally replaces the typical *dendê* oil, however, with a different oil called *urucu(m),* made from the berries of the annatto tree. There is also a famous seasoned pie called *torta capixaba,* traditionally made at Easter time, which contains fish, shellfish and seafood mixed with palm hearts and covered with beaten eggs.

Ceramic pot from *Ilha do Marajó,* or Marajó Island. It is a replica of the pottery made by of the oldest Indian cultures in South America, and is characterized by its distinctive geometric pattern.

Paraná

Santa Catarina

Rio Grande do Sul

THE SOUTHERN REGION OF BRAZIL

THE SOUTH

The three states of Paraná, Santa Catarina and Rio Grande do Sul comprise the southern region of Brazil. In this part of the country there are two quite disparate traditions, that of the cowboy, or *gaúcho,* on the large cattle ranches or *estâncias,* and that of the immigrant homesteader. Both provided unique contributions to Brazilian cookery.

In colonial times, the grasslands, or *pampas,* of the south were inhabited by indigenous people and Portuguese settlers. This region is a part of present-day Rio Grande do Sul, the southernmost state of Brazil, but the grasslands continue through Uruguay and into Argentina. Since few women accompanied the early settlers to the new world, miscegenation between the colonists and the Indians inevitably occurred. Their descendents, vigorous and hardy frontiersmen who came to be known as *gaúchos,* hunted wild cattle derived from the herds brought to the South American plains by the Spaniards. At the same time, they protected the Portuguese Crown's southern borders from encroachment by the neighboring Spanish. Initially, only cattle hides were important, but later, when the land had been subdivided into the great *estâncias,* meat also became a valuable commodity and an enormous cattle industry developed. The meat from these ranches supplied food for the miners during the great gold rush in Minas Gerais, Goias and Mato Grosso in the late seventeenth century and for the laborers on the coffee plantations, or *fazendas,* during the coffee boom in the state of São Paulo in the mid-nineteenth century.

Without refrigeration, much of the meat was preserved by salting and sun-drying. *Carne do sol,* or *charque,* as this meat was known, resisted spoilage, even in the tropics, and was enjoyed throughout the country, as it is today. A popular and tasty dish in Rio Grande do Sul prepared with this dried meat is *arroz de carreteiro,* or "wagoner's rice." It is a mixture of rice, small pieces of rehydrated dried meat, often with tomato and green pepper added, topped with chopped parsley and scallions and given a bit of a bite with hot *malagueta* peppers. Small pieces of fried sweet manioc, called *aipim frita,* and the sweet pumpkin confection known as *doce de abóbora* are also representative of the area.

The *gaúchos* gave to the cuisine of Brazil the *churrasco,* a veritable orgy of fresh, spit-grilled barbecued meat. It became an extension of the usual way they prepared their meals out in the open. Gigantic slabs of meat, bones and all, and large coils of *lingüiça* sausage are put on hefty skewers and grilled over hot embers of wood. Salt in the form of a brine is brushed on the surface of the meat to seal in moisture. A sauce called *molho campanha,* made of chopped onion, tomato and green pepper steeped in wine vinegar, traditionally accompanies this dish. Typically, pieces of grilled meat are dipped in manioc meal before eating. The *churrasco* moved indoors in the cities, and many restaurants, or *churrascarias,* in the south and throughout Brazil specialize in this showy feast.

Although most of the country became addicted to drinking coffee, the *gaúchos* preferred their unsweetened, tea-like beverage called *chimmarão* derived from the leaves of an indigenous plant called *erva mate.* Their interesting ritual was to put the dried leaves, or *mate,* into a small, sometimes elaborately decorated gourd known as a *cuia,* add boiling water, and when steeped, drink the somewhat bitter concoction with a silver straw, or *bomba.* It was strong stuff. Several refills were possible without changing leaves, and the contents of the gourd often were shared among friends. This paraphernalia for drinking *chimmarão* was a part of the traditional gear of the *gaúcho.* He was a distinctive figure, both astride his horse and around the *churrasco* fires. He dressed in baggy pants called *bombaches* that were tied at the bottom, wore a linen shirt, a bandana around his neck, a broad-rimmed hat and carried a knife held in place by his wide leather belt. His boots were of leather with a generous cut that caused the material to drape in loose folds beginning at the ankle and continuing on up toward the top. Present day *gaúchos* still call the grassy plains of Rio Grande do Sul home, but the term has become a generic one to mean all residents of the state.

Besides the rich grazing lands of the *pampas,* the south has hilly, even mountainous regions, and forests. This area became home to millions of immigrants after Brazil became an independent nation in 1822 and the virtually empty land there was made available for settlement. The largest groups to colonize the southern states were the Italians and Germans, but sizable groups of Poles and Russians also came, all bringing their strong work ethic and a desire to establish self-sufficiency through their independent farming endeavors. Other groups poured into the south from the present-day state of São Paulo after giving work on the coffee plantations a try, and the colonies grew prosperous. They were isolated from each other by virtue of the enormity of the land, slowing the process of assimilation. For a long time, the Germans in particular actively resisted assimilation, but today only a few isolated villages remain more German than Brazilian.

The diet of the immigrants was wheat-based. Another customary staple was the potato, but when that was unavailable the native sweet manioc tuber called *aipim* or *macaxeira* was a reasonable substitute. The larder also contained meat, dairy products and garden produce, adding leafy green vegetables to the Brazilian diet, a food previously considered unimportant. Thus the immigrants had at hand a variety of familiar foods, enabling them to nearly reproduce their traditional dishes. They had little need to improvise with native ingredients as had the Portuguese settlers centuries earlier. Their contribution to Brazilian cuisine was a taste of Europe.

Throughout the south one can sample the popular ethnic foods by seeking out the particular regions where various immigrant groups settled. Several of these cities strive to maintain the European style of architecture that the early colonists carried over to the new land and to keep the folklore alive. The cities of Blumenau, Joinville and especially Pomerode, in Santa Catarina, have an old-world German aura. Many of the buildings resemble alpine chalets with steep roofs and half-timbered facades. Of more recent vintage is an enormously successful Oktoberfest celebration held annually in Blumenau. It is based on the Bavarian harvest festival involving much merrymaking, beer drinking and sausage eating. Another such festival occurs in Nova Petrópolis, one of the cities in Rio Grande do Sul with strong Germanic roots. Wine festivals and Italian heritage are especially prominent in the towns of Caxias do Sul and Bento Gonçalves. In Paraná, the heritage of the Slavic immigrants is much in evidence in the city of Prudentópolis.

Tastes of Brazil

You are encouraged to try some of these classic Brazilian recipes before you leave home. This is a wonderful and immediately rewarding way to preview the extraordinary cuisine of Brazil. Most of the special Brazilian ingredients necessary for these recipes are available in the United States (see *Resources*, p. 61). Satisfactory substitutes are given for unavailable ones.

If you enjoy wine with your meal, be sure to try some imported Brazilian wine from the vineyards in the south. Descendants of Italian immigrants in the state of Rio Grande do Sul produce excellent wine. The Marcus James label is inexpensive and readily available in the United States. Varieties to choose from include cabernet sauvignon, merlot, white zinfandel, chardonnay and a dry riesling.

You may want to try some of the many drinks made with imported Brazilian brandy, or *cachaça*. Recipes for the two most popular *cachaça* drinks are included.

APPETIZERS

Bolinhos de Arroz

Little rice balls. Makes about 12.
Deise Dutra, São Paulo, provided the recipe for this appetizer *(salgadinho)* which uses leftover rice.

> 1 EGG, LIGHTLY BEATEN
>
> 1 SMALL ONION, FINELY CHOPPED
>
> 1 GREEN SCALLION, FINELY CHOPPED
>
> 1 TABLESPOON FRESH PARSLEY, CHOPPED
>
> 3–4 TABLESPOONS FLOUR
>
> ½ TEASPOON SALT
>
> 1 TABLESPOON MILK

[Bolinhos de Arroz, *continued*]

    1 CUP LEFTOVER RICE

    VEGETABLE OIL FOR FRYING

Mix together the egg, onion, scallion, parsley, flour, milk and salt. Add rice. Fry rounded tablespoons of the batter in hot oil until golden brown. Drain on absorbent paper.

Empadinhas de Galinha

Small, savory pastries filled with chicken and vegetables. Plan ahead—the chicken needs to marinate 1 hour. Makes about 18.

This recipe for a popular appetizer (*salgadinho*) enjoyed throughout the country was provided by June Parreiras, Viçosa, Minas Gerais.

Dough

    ⅜ CUP BUTTER

    ⅛ CUP SHORTENING

    2¾ CUP FLOUR

    1 TEASPOON SALT

    3 EGG YOLKS

    2–3 TABLESPOONS COLD WATER

Blend together the butter, shortening, flour and salt. Add the egg yolks, saving a small amount to brush on top of the *empadinhas* before baking. Add water as needed to make a pastry. Set dough aside while preparing the filling.

Filling

    JUICE OF 1 LEMON

    1 CLOVE GARLIC, MINCED

    2 SMALL ONIONS, CHOPPED

    4 SCALLIONS, CHOPPED

    4 TABLESPOONS FRESH PARSLEY, CHOPPED

    1 *MALAGUETA* PEPPER, FINELY CHOPPED*

    SALT AND PEPPER TO TASTE

    2–3 CHICKEN BREASTS, BONED OR UNBONED

    2–3 TABLESPOONS VEGETABLE OIL

    ½ CUP WATER

¼ POUND FROZEN CORN, COOKED

¼ POUND FROZEN PEAS, COOKED

⅓ CUP GREEN OLIVES, FINELY CHOPPED

⅓ CUP CARROTS, COOKED AND FINELY CHOPPED

¾ CUP POTATOES, COOKED AND CUT INTO SMALL CUBES

1 CUP MILK

1 TABLESPOON FLOUR

Prepare a marinade *(vinha d'alho)* by blending together the lemon juice, garlic, 1 onion, 2 scallions, parsley, *malagueta* pepper, salt and black pepper. Marinate the chicken breasts for 1 hour. Pour off the marinade and set aside. Fry the chicken in 1–2 tablespoons oil, browning it on both sides. Add the reserved marinade and water, cover, and cook until done. Add more water, if necessary. Remove the chicken and shred it into fine pieces when cool. Sauté remaining scallions and onion in the rest of the oil until limp. Return the shredded chicken to the frying pan. Add the corn, peas, green olives, carrots and potatoes. Blend together the flour and the milk. Add this mixture to the filling and cook until thickened. Set aside.

Roll out the pastry as thin as possible and cut out rounds sufficiently large to cover the bottom and sides of the wells of a lightly-greased, shallow muffin pan. Stuff ¾ full with the filling. Cover each with a circle of rolled pastry and press the tops and sides together to seal. Brush the tops with the reserved egg yolk and bake at 375°F for 35–45 minutes until done.

*Malagueta peppers are chilies. They should be handled carefully because they contain oils that can irritate or burn the skin or eyes. In the United States, they are available bottled, not fresh. See *Resources* (p. 61) for mail-order suppliers.

Coxinhas

Mock chicken legs. Makes about 15.

This appetizer, or *salgadinho*, is popular throughout Brazil.

1 3-POUND CHICKEN, CUT INTO PIECES

3 TABLESPOONS OLIVE OIL

3 CLOVES GARLIC, MINCED

1 MEDIUM ONION, CHOPPED

1 BAY LEAF

SALT AND PEPPER TO TASTE

1 CUP RICE FLOUR

[Coxinhas, *continued*]

> 2 CUPS MILK
>
> 1 CUP RESERVED CHICKEN BROTH
>
> 3 EGG YOLKS, BEATEN
>
> 1 TABLESPOON BUTTER
>
> 1 *MALAGUETA* PEPPER, FINELY CHOPPED*
>
> 4 CUPS FINE BREAD CRUMBS
>
> 2 EGGS, BEATEN
>
> VEGETABLE OIL FOR FRYING

Sauté the chicken in olive oil. Add garlic, onion, bay leaf, salt and pepper to taste. Cover with water and simmer until done. Remove chicken and reserve 1 cup broth. Take the meat off the bones. Reserve 15 thin strips of chicken and finely chop the remainder. Whisk together the flour, milk and reserved broth until smooth and cook over medium heat until thickened, stirring constantly. Remove from heat and stir in egg yolks, butter, chicken and *malagueta* pepper. Correct the seasonings. Return to heat and stir until quite thick. Completely cool mixture in refrigerator. Take an amount the size of a large egg and shape it around a reserved strip of chicken, forming a "drumstick." Roll in bread crumbs, dip into beaten eggs and cover with another layer of bread crumbs. Fry in hot oil until golden brown.

Note: a bone from the cooked chicken can be placed into each *coxinha*, along with the strip of chicken meat, providing a closer resemblance to a chicken leg.

*Malagueta peppers are chilies. They should be handled carefully because they contain oils that can irritate or burn the skin or eyes. In the United States, they are available bottled, not fresh. See *Resources* (p. 61) for mail-order suppliers.

Main Dishes

Camarão na Moranga

Winter squash with shrimp. Serves 8.

Circe Zugno, Coari, Amazonas, contributed her favorite recipe.

> 1 WINTER SQUASH, MEDIUM
>
> 3 TABLESPOONS OIL
>
> 2 POUNDS MEDIUM-SIZE SHRIMP, DEVEINED
>
> 8 JUMBO SHRIMP FOR DECORATION, DEVEINED
>
> SALT AND WHITE PEPPER TO TASTE
>
> JUICE OF 1 LEMON

2 TABLESPOONS BUTTER

2 ONIONS, CHOPPED

1 TEASPOON SWEET PAPRIKA

1 TEASPOON MUSTARD POWDER (OR 2 TEASPOONS PREPARED MUSTARD)

6 TABLESPOONS COGNAC

2 TEASPOONS FLOUR

2 CUPS CREAM

1¾ CUP CREAM CHEESE, SOFTENED*

Coordinate preparation of the squash and shrimp. Cut off and discard the top of the squash, remove all seeds and stringy fibers and rub the outside surface with 2 tablespoons oil. Bake 1 hour at 250°F. The squash will not darken appreciably during this time.

While the squash is baking, season the shrimp with salt and white pepper to taste and sprinkle with lemon juice. Heat the butter and the remaining oil in a pan and fry the onions until limp but not dark. Add the shrimp, including the jumbo shrimp, and sauté until pink, approximately 2 minutes on each side. Remove the jumbo shrimp and set aside. Season the remaining shrimp with paprika and mustard. Remove the pan from the stove, pour the cognac on the shrimp mixture and flame it. When the flames are out, return the pan to the stove. Mix the flour with the cream and add it to the shrimp mixture. Stir over low heat until thickened. Add the cream cheese and continue to stir over low heat until the cheese is melted. Correct the seasonings.

Remove the squash from the oven to a serving plate. Pour the shrimp mixture into the squash. Decorate the rim of the squash with the reserved jumbo shrimp. Serve with white rice.

*The recipe calls for *requeijão cremoso,* a creamy cheese not available in the United States. Cream cheese is a reasonable substitute.

Moqueca de Camarão

Shrimp stew, Bahian style. Serves 4. Plan ahead—the shrimp needs to marinate for 30 minutes.

JUICE OF 1 LEMON

1 ONION, FINELY CHOPPED

1 CLOVE GARLIC, MINCED

1–2 TABLESPOONS WHITE VINEGAR

½ TEASPOON SALT

[Moqueca de Camarão, *continued*]

> 1 POUND FRESH SHRIMP, SHELLED AND DEVEINED
>
> 1 TEASPOON FRESH CILANTRO, CHOPPED
>
> 2 TABLESPOONS TOMATO PASTE
>
> BLACK PEPPER TO TASTE
>
> 1 CUP THIN COCONUT MILK*
>
> ½ CUP THICK COCONUT MILK*
>
> 2–3 TABLESPOONS *DENDÊ* OIL

Make a marinade *(vinha d'alho)* with lemon, onion, garlic, vinegar and salt. Marinate the shrimp for 30 minutes. Put mixture into a sauce pan and add cilantro, tomato paste and black pepper to taste. Add thin coconut milk and cook over low heat until the shrimp are cooked. Add the thick coconut milk and *dendê* oil. Continue cooking for another 5 minutes. Serve with rice.

*See p. 53; bottled or canned coconut milk can be substituted.

Galinhada

Rice with chicken. Plan ahead—the chicken needs to marinate 1 hour. Serves 6. This recipe, typical of the center-west region, was provided by Jane Ambrosio, Brasília, Distrito Federal.

> JUICE OF 2 LEMONS
>
> 1 CLOVE GARLIC, MINCED
>
> 2 SMALL ONIONS, CHOPPED
>
> 2 SCALLIONS, CHOPPED
>
> 2 TABLESPOONS FRESH PARSLEY, COARSELY CHOPPED
>
> 1 *MALAGUETA* PEPPER, FINELY CHOPPED*
>
> SALT
>
> PEPPER
>
> 2 POUNDS CHICKEN, CUT INTO PIECES
>
> 1 CUP RICE
>
> ½ POUND FROZEN CORN, COOKED
>
> ½ CUP BLACK OLIVES, SLICED
>
> 3–4 TABLESPOONS VEGETABLE OIL
>
> SAFFRON, PINCH

Prepare a marinade *(vinha d'alho)* by mixing together the lemon juice, garlic, 1 onion, 1 scallion, parsley, *malagueta* pepper, and salt and black pepper to taste. Marinate the chicken for 1 hour, turning occasionally. Drain the chicken, reserving the marinade, and brown it in a frying pan in half the oil. Cover the browned chicken with the reserved marinade, adding water if necessary, and simmer until cooked. Remove the chicken and coarsely shred it when cool. Set aside. Reserve the broth. Heat the remaining oil, add 1 onion and scallion and fry until limp. Add the uncooked rice and mix until coated with oil but not browned. Mix in the shredded chicken, corn, olives and saffron; correct the seasonings. Add 2 cups of the reserved chicken broth; add water if necessary to make 2 cups. Cook until rice is of the desired consistency.

Note: a variation of this dish often contains the *pequi* fruit (souari nut) from a tree common to the center-west part of the country. The fruit imparts a distinct flavor to the dish, called *galinhada com pequi*. Since *pequi* is not readily available in the United States, look for *galinhada com pequi* on menus in the center-west region to compare its flavor with plain *galinhada* above. (When preparing *pequi* for this dish, one must be very careful to remove the sharp thorns in the seed case.)

Malagueta peppers are chilies. They should be handled carefully because they contain oils that can irritate or burn the skin or eyes. In the United States, they are available bottled, not fresh. See *Resources* (p. 61) for mail-order suppliers.

Arroz de Carreteiro

Wagoner's rice. Serves 10. Plan ahead—the meat needs to soak overnight in water. This recipe, typical of the southern region, was contributed by Corália Medeiros, São Francisco de Assis, Rio Grande do Sul.

> 2 POUNDS DRIED, SALTED BEEF *(CARNE SECA*)*
>
> 5 SMALL CLOVES GARLIC, MINCED
>
> 3 SMALL ONIONS, CHOPPED
>
> 2–3 TABLESPOONS VEGETABLE OIL
>
> 2 CUPS RICE
>
> 4 CUPS WATER (TO COOK RICE)
>
> SALT
>
> BLACK PEPPER
>
> ½ CUP PARSLEY, CHOPPED
>
> ½ CUP SCALLIONS, CHOPPED
>
> CAYENNE PEPPER (OPTIONAL)

[Arroz de Carreteiro, *continued*]

Cut meat into small cubes, about ½ inch on each side. Cover with water and soak overnight or boil for 15 minutes, to rehydrate the meat and remove the salt. Drain. Fry the onion and garlic in oil until limp. Add meat and fry until browned. Add salt, black pepper and cayenne pepper to taste. Mix in rice and cook 5 minutes. Add boiling water and boil for 2 minutes. Cover and simmer until the rice is of the desired consistency. Top with parsley and scallions.

*See *Resources* (p. 61) for mail-order suppliers.

Frango Imperial

Chicken Imperial. Serves 6. Plan ahead—the chicken needs to marinate overnight.

This recipe of Portuguese origin was provided by Leticia Anand, formerly of São Paulo.

> 1 3-POUND CHICKEN, SKINNED AND CUT INTO PIECES
>
> ¼ CUP RED WINE VINEGAR
>
> 1 CLOVE GARLIC, MINCED
>
> SALT AND PEPPER TO TASTE
>
> 1 CUP PARMESAN CHEESE, FRESHLY GRATED
>
> 1 MEDIUM ONION, GRATED
>
> 2–3 TABLESPOONS BUTTER
>
> PORT WINE

Make a marinade *(vinha d'alho)* with vinegar, garlic, salt and pepper. Marinate the chicken overnight. Then dry the pieces well with absorbent paper and roll in grated cheese. Place in a baking dish with onions and dots of butter. Bake in a preheated oven at 375°F for 45–50 minutes or until golden. Reduce temperature to 325°F and lightly douse each piece with a little wine. Bake until chicken is cooked.

Cuscuz Paulista

Molded shrimp couscous, São Paulo style. Plan ahead—the shrimp needs to marinate 1 hour. Serves 12.

This dish, typical of the state of São Paulo in the southeastern region, was provided by Emilia Martins Mateus, São Paulo. This version eliminates the need for steaming the mixture in a special container, or *cuscuzeiro.*

> JUICE OF 2 LEMONS
>
> 2 CLOVES GARLIC, MINCED

SALT

PEPPER

1 POUND MEDIUM-SIZED SHRIMP, FRESH

2½ CUPS CORNMEAL

2 TABLESPOONS MANIOC FLOUR (MEAL)

1 CUP BOILING WATER CONTAINING 1 TABLESPOON SALT

½ CUP OLIVE OIL OR MELTED BUTTER

1 4-OUNCE CAN SARDINES IN OIL (NO BONES OR SCALES)

3 TOMATOES (1 SLICED; 2 SEEDED AND CHOPPED)

1 EGG, HARD-BOILED AND SLICED

½ CUP PITTED BLACK OLIVES

¾ CUP CANNED HEARTS OF PALM, SLICED INTO ROUNDS
     (RESERVE THE LIQUID)

1 LARGE ONION, CHOPPED

3 SCALLIONS, CHOPPED

1 BAY LEAF

¾ CUP FROZEN PEAS, COOKED

Make a marinade (*vinha d'alho*) with lemon juice, 1 clove garlic, salt and pepper to taste. Marinate the shrimp for 1 hour. Combine the cornmeal and manioc meal and toast in a preheated oven (300°F) for 5 minutes, shaking pan occasionally. Add salted, boiling water and mix well. Stir in ¼ cup melted butter or olive oil. Set aside.

Lightly grease a bowl (or line it with cheesecloth). To garnish the surface of the *cuscuz,* place 3 sardines on the bottom of the bowl. Put slices of tomato, hard-boiled eggs, olives and palm hearts on the bottom and up the sides of the bowl, reserving room for a few cooked shrimp (see below). In a large frying pan, sauté the onion and remaining garlic in ¼ cup melted butter or olive oil. Add scallions and the remaining tomatoes. Mix in shrimp, the marinade and bay leaf. Simmer 15–20 minutes. Remove 4 or 5 shrimp, cut in half lengthwise, and add to garnish in bowl. Stir in the peas and the remaining hearts of palm, olives and sardines. Correct the seasonings. Blend in the cornmeal/manioc mixture and stir over medium heat for 15–20 minutes. The mixture should have a paste-like consistency. If too dry, add some liquid from the can of palm hearts.

Pour some of the mixture into the bowl and press down firmly to hold the garnish in place. Fill the bowl with the rest of the mixture, again pressing firmly. Let sit a few minutes and unmold by inverting over a plate. Use an oiled knife to cut into pieces. Serve immediately.

Peixe Ensopado

Fish stew. Plan ahead—the fish needs to marinate 1–3 hours. Serves 4.

Stews flavored with coconut are called *ensopados.* This version is made with fish. Anisia Quirino da Silva, Rio de Janeiro, provided this delicious recipe. Anisia uses *badejo,* a fish similar to sea bass. A good substitute is haddock.

> JUICE OF ONE LIME
>
> ½ TEASPOON SALT
>
> BLACK PEPPER TO TASTE
>
> 4 FISH STEAKS
>
> 1 LARGE ONION, CHOPPED
>
> 1 CLOVE GARLIC, MINCED
>
> 8 GREEN OLIVES, SLICED
>
> 3 TABLESPOONS FRESH CILANTRO, CHOPPED
>
> 2 TABLESPOONS OLIVE OIL*
>
> 2 TABLESPOONS TOMATO PASTE
>
> 1 *MALAGUETA* PEPPER, CHOPPED (OPTIONAL)†
>
> ½ CUP COCONUT MILK††

Prepare a marinade *(vinha d'alho)* of lime juice, salt and pepper. Marinate the fish for 1–3 hours. Sauté the onion, olives and garlic in oil until onion is limp. Mix in cilantro and cook for 1 minute. Add fish and marinade. Simmer 10–15 minutes, or until fish is done. Mix in tomato paste, *malagueta* pepper and coconut milk. Simmer for another 5 minutes. Serve with rice.

* For a different flavor, replace 1 tablespoon of olive oil with *dendê* oil. The stew would then be a *moqueca,* typical of the northeastern region.

†*Malagueta* peppers are chilies. They should be handled carefully because they contain oils that can irritate or burn the skin or eyes. In the United States, they are available bottled, not fresh. See *Resources* (p. 61) for mail-order suppliers.

†† See p. 53; bottled or canned coconut milk can be substitued.

Picadinho de Porco

Minced pork. Serves 6.

This recipe is a variation of the popular dish called *picadinho* made with minced beef.

> 1 TABLESPOON BUTTER OR BACON FAT
>
> 1 ONION, FINELY CHOPPED

2 TOMATOES, PEELED, SEEDED AND DICED

2 POUNDS PORK, FINELY CHOPPED

½ POUND SMOKED *CHOURIÇO* SAUSAGE (SMOKED ANDOUILLE OR
    KIELBASA SAUSAGE CAN BE SUBSTITUTED)

JUICE OF 1 LEMON

SALT

BLACK PEPPER

2 EGGS, HARD-BOILED AND SLICED

2 TABLESPOONS FRESH PARSLEY, MINCED

1 *MALAGUETA* PEPPER, CHOPPED (OPTIONAL)*

Sauté onion in butter or bacon fat until softened. Add tomatoes and stir over medium heat until thickened. Add the pork and the sausage, after removing the casing. Mix well, breaking the sausage into small pieces. Cook for 20–25 minutes, or until the meat is done. Stir in lemon juice and *malagueta* pepper, salt and black pepper to taste. Cook over low heat for 5 minutes. Transfer to serving bowl and garnish with egg slices and parsley

Malagueta peppers are chilies. They should be handled carefully because they contain oils that can irritate or burn the skin or eyes. In the United States, they are available bottled, not fresh. See *Resources* (p. 61) for mail-order suppliers.

VEGETABLES

Couve à Mineira

Kale in the style of Minas Gerais. Serves 6.

This vegetable dish traditionally accompanies several regional dishes of Minas Gerais and Brazil's national dish, *feijoada*.

    1 POUND KALE

    1 CLOVE GARLIC, MINCED

    1 MEDIUM ONION, CHOPPED

    2 TABLESPOONS OLIVE OIL

Wash and drain kale thoroughly. Bunch the leaves together and cut into thin strips. Sauté the garlic and onion in oil. Add kale and cook over moderate heat for about 5 minutes. Kale should be soft but not discolored.

Note: broccoli leaves make a delicious substitute for kale.

SIDE DISHES

Farofa de Manteiga

Buttered manioc meal. Serves 4.

This recipe is one of many ways plain manioc meal can be embellished with flavorful ingredients.

> 2–3 TABLESPOONS VEGETABLE OIL
>
> 1 SMALL ONION, COARSELY CHOPPED
>
> 1 EGG
>
> 1 CUP MANIOC MEAL
>
> 2 TABLESPOONS FRESH PARSLEY, MINCED
>
> SALT AND PEPPER TO TASTE

Sauté onion in butter until soft, but not browned. Reduce heat and add egg, stirring until scrambled and well mixed. Gradually add manioc meal until the mixture becomes golden and resembles toasted bread crumbs. Add salt and pepper and stir in parsley.

Vatapá

Spicy, creamed shrimp and nuts. Serves 8.

This is the most famous of the mashes or purées created by the African slaves during colonial times in the northeastern region of Brazil. It is a side dish served with rice or a filling for the fried bean fritters called *acarajé*.

> ¼ POUND STALE WHITE BREAD CUBES
>
> 1½ CUPS THICK COCONUT MILK*
>
> ⅓ CUP ROASTED PEANUTS, FINELY GROUND
>
> ⅓ CUP CASHEWS, FINELY GROUND
>
> 1 CUP DRIED SMOKED SHRIMP, SHELLED AND PULVERIZED†
>
> 1 SMALL ONION, MINCED
>
> 1 CLOVE GARLIC, MINCED
>
> 1–2 *MALAGUETA* PEPPERS, CHOPPED††
>
> 1 TEASPOON FRESH GINGER, MINCED
>
> ½ CUP THIN COCONUT MILK OR WATER
>
> ¼ CUP *DÊNDE* OIL
>
> SALT TO TASTE

Soak bread cubes in thick coconut milk in a food processor until softened. Blend well, then remove to saucepan. Add remaining ingredients except *dendê* oil. Simmer over low heat until thick, stirring constantly. If mixture is too stiff, add more thin coconut milk or water. Add oil and salt to taste and stir well. To obtain proper consistency, the nuts and shrimp must be very finely ground.

*See p. 53; bottled or canned coconut milk can be substituted.

†Dried, unsmoked shrimp, can be substituted for the more pungent smoked ones, but the taste will be different. See *Resources* (p. 61) for mail-order sources of Brazilian foods.

††*Malagueta* peppers are chillies. Handle them carefully because they contain oils that can irritate or burn the skin or eyes. In the United States, they are available bottled, not fresh. See *Resources* (p. 61) for mail-order sources of Brazilian foods.

Arroz Brasileiro

Brazilian-style rice. Serves 8.

> 2 TABLESPOONS VEGETABLE OIL
>
> 1 SMALL ONION, CHOPPED
>
> 1 CLOVE GARLIC, MINCED
>
> 2 TOMATOES, CHOPPED
>
> 2 CUPS RICE, UNCOOKED
>
> 4 CUPS BOILING WATER
>
> 1 TEASPOON SALT

Combine oil, onion, garlic, tomatoes and rice. Sauté for 5 minutes. (This is the *refogado** process). Add salt to boiling water and pour over rice. Bring to a boil, cover and reduce heat. Simmer until water has been absorbed, about 20 minutes.

*a preliminary step in Brazilian cooking which involves lightly sautéeing in a mixture of oil, onion, tomatoes, garlic and seasonings. When this technique is used with rice, the individual grains become well-seasoned and do not stick together.

BREADS/ROLLS

Pão de Queijo

Cheese Rolls. Makes 12.

These rolls are especially popular in the center-west, southeastern and southern regions of Brazil.

> 1 CUP TAPIOCA STARCH
>
> ¼ CUP VEGETABLE OIL

[Pão de Queijo, *continued*]

> ¼ CUP WATER
>
> 1 TEASPOON SALT
>
> 1 EGG
>
> 6 TABLESPOONS PLAIN YOGURT, NONFAT OR REGULAR
>
> 1 CUP GRATED PARMESAN CHEESE

Preheat oven to 450°F. Put tapioca starch in a metal bowl. Mix oil, water and salt in a pan. Bring to a boil. Pour the sputtering mixture onto the tapioca starch carefully to protect yourself from hot spatters. Mix together with a wooden spoon. Dough will be stiff. When cool enough to touch, add egg and mix well. Blend in yogurt. When well mixed, stir in cheese. Rub hands with oil and form batter into balls. Place on a greased baking sheet. Reduce oven temperature to 350°F. Bake 25–30 minutes.

DESSERTS

Quindim de Yá-Yá*

Young girl's dessert. Makes about 16 cakes.

The recipe for this dessert, typical of the northeastern region, was provided by Fatima Silverio, Raul Soares, Minas Gerais.

> ¼ POUND BUTTER, SOFTENED
>
> 1½ CUPS SUGAR
>
> 9 EGG YOLKS
>
> 1 CUP COCONUT, FRESHLY GRATED

Preheat oven to 350°F. Cream the butter and sugar, mixing well. Add the egg yolks, one by one, stirring well after each addition. The sugar must be completely dissolved. Add the coconut and blend without beating. Lightly grease a shallow muffin pan and fill each well to a depth of 1 inch. Set the filled muffin pan into a baking tray containing about ½ inch of water and bake for about 35 minutes. Make sure the water does not boil over into the muffin pan. The *quindins* will be lightly browned on the surface. Cool. Carefully loosen the edges with a knife before inverting the muffin pan over a flat surface to unmold the cakes. The top of the *quindins* are golden yellow and have a gelatin-like consistency. The bases are like coconut macaroons.*

*During colonial times in the northeastern region, the young girls of the plantation mansions, or *casas grandes,* were addressed as Yá-Yá by the slaves.

Mugunzá

Hominy dessert. Serves 10.

Mugunzá is one of the dishes traditionally eaten throughout Brazil during the winter festival called *Festa Junina*. This recipe was provided by Martha Laboissiere, Brasília, Distrito Federal.

> 2 15-OUNCE CANS WHITE HOMINY
>
> 1½ CUPS WHOLE MILK
>
> ¾ CAN SWEETENED CONDENSED MILK
>
> 1 CUP THICK COCONUT MILK*
>
> ¾ CUP UNSALTED PEANUTS, ROASTED AND GROUND
>
> CINNAMON (OPTIONAL)

Wash and drain hominy. Add milk and cook over low heat for 20 minutes or until hominy is soft, stirring occasionally. Add condensed milk, coconut milk and peanuts. Simmer for another 10 minutes, stirring occasionally. Transfer mixture into a serving bowl. Chill. Serve with cinnamon sprinkled on top.

*See p. 53; bottled or canned coconut milk can be substituted.

MISCELLANEOUS

Coconut Milk

Coconut meat and the milk made from it are key components in Brazilian cookery. It is easy to make coconut milk from freshly grated coconut and capture the authentic taste of Brazilian dishes using it. A thick, rich milk is produced from the first squeezing of the gratings; a thinner milk is derived from a second round of squeezing.

> 1 COCONUT*
>
> ½ CUP WARM WATER (FOR THICK MILK)
>
> 2–3 CUPS WARM WATER (FOR THIN MILK)

Heat the coconut in a preheated oven (350°F) for 10 minutes to crack the coconut. Remove the coconut from the oven (with potholders!) and place it in a large metal bowl on the floor. Cover the bowl with a towel and hit the coconut with a hammer to break it completely open. More than one strike may be necessary. Remove the pieces of broken coconut from the bowl. Strain the coconut water (*agua de côco*) that is released through a coffee filter to remove any fibers, and set aside. Separate the coconut meat from the shell, using a dull knife to pry them apart if necessary.

[Coconut milk, *continued*]

Remove the brown skin from the coconut meat with a vegetable peeler and grate the meat in a food processor.

To make the thick milk, put the gratings into cheesecloth or a clean white dish towel and hold the ends together. Soak the wrapped gratings in ½ cup warm water in a small bowl for a few minutes. Firmly squeeze the gratings over the bowl. About ¾ cup of thick milk will be obtained. A less efficient method of making thick coconut milk is to put the grated coconut in a sieve, wet it with warm water, and press out the milk with a spoon.

Thin milk is made by soaking the same wrapped gratings in 2–3 cups of warm water and repeating the squeezing procedure. (Use the reserved coconut water and bring the volume to 2–3 cups with warm water.)

Canned or bottled coconut milk can be purchased at specialty stores. Dishes made with it, however, will not have the authentic Brazilian taste that is provided by freshly prepared coconut milk.

*Before buying a coconut, shake it to make sure it contains water.

CLASSIC BRAZILIAN DRINKS

Caipirinha

Brandy cocktail named "little peasant girl." Serves 1.

This famous drink is made with *cachaça,* the fiery brandy made from Brazilian sugar cane. The *caipirinha* traditionally contains chunks of tart, green Brazilian lemon, a fruit more like our lime. It is enormously popular.

> 1 LIME, QUARTERED
>
> 1–2 TABLESPOONS SUGAR
>
> 2 OUNCES *CACHAÇA**
>
> ICE CUBES

Mash the lime quarters in a cocktail glass with a wooden pestle.† Do not remove the pieces of crushed lime. Add the sugar and *cachaça*. Fill the glass with ice cubes and stir well.

Cachaça is available in the the United States in metropolitan liquor stores and in some Brazilian specialty food stores. See *Resources* (p. 61) for mail-order suppliers. In Brazil, visit the museum, Museo do Homen do Nordeste, in Recife, to see the exhibit devoted to the history of *cachaça* production.

†A variety of pestles are on sale in Brazilian markets. Some are ornately carved and make great souvenirs.

Batida

The batida is a cooler traditionally made with fruit juice, especially tropical fruit juice, and *cachaça*. Serves 1.

3–4 OUNCES FRUIT JUICE

2 OUNCES *CACHAÇA*

SUGAR TO TASTE

4 OUNCES CRUSHED ICE

Mix the ingredients together in a blender and blend until smooth. Pour into a cocktail glass.

Shopping in Brazil's Food Markets

Helpful Tips

The Open-Air Markets

Learning more about Brazilian food in the outdoor market setting is fascinating. Dozens of unusual fruits and vegetables are available nowhere else. Many of the markets, or *mercados,* in the smaller towns are centrally located and commonly held on a specific day of the week. Market day, or *dia de feira,* is an important social event whose tradition can be traced to the Portuguese. They named the weekdays as market days, beginning with Monday, which was called *segunda feira,* or second market, and ending with Friday, called *sexta feira,* or sixth market.

To get a feeling for how purchases are negotiated, stroll around the rows of food stalls and watch the lively interaction between the vendors and the local people. You will note that the prices typically are firm but will vary a bit between vendors. Prices usually are marked, but if not, it would be wise to see what the local folk pay so you don't end up paying a lot more.

Food in the markets is sold either by weight (kilogram) or by quantity (small batches called *lotes,* often neatly bundled in plastic fish-netting). To encourage sales, the vendors offer generous samples to taste. This is a good opportunity to ask for the name of an item that is not labelled. If you would like to give Portuguese a try, see *Helpful Phrases* (p. 65). The vendors, and many of the other Brazilians around you, will be happy to answer questions. In fact, questions are anticipated for the medicines, potions and other curatives that are also available in many outdoor markets.

To me, the most astounding items in these markets, especially in the north and northeastern parts of the country, are the exotic fruits. Their flavors are unique and distinctive. You will note in the *Foods & Flavors Guide* that I likened some of these new tastes to those of known fruit whenever I felt I could detect a similarity. Taste is so subjective that you will have to try some of them to see if you agree with me!

Many of the fresh fruits are made into delicious juices. While some juices *(sucos)* are for sale at the outdoor markets, most of the produce has not been processed. A better selection of juices is available at fruit bars. You can't miss these places; many varieties of fruit are prominently displayed in the windows to entice you. An added bonus is that the out-of-season fruits are available as frozen pulps.

A Health Precaution

Don't ask for trouble. Some serious diseases such as dysentary, giardia, hepatitis, typhoid and cholera can be transmitted by eating unwashed produce. Avoid eating food from street vendors. Some serious diseases can be transmitted by eating unclean produce. If you buy fruits and vegetables in the markets, make sure to wash them thoroughly with bottled water before eating. The safest fruits are those that can be peeled. Bottled water is readily available and is a wise choice, even in restaurants. Also, always brush your teeth with bottled water.

As mentioned in the *Foods & Flavors Guide*, some types of fruit are never eaten raw. If you find varieties not in my list, it would be wise to inquire whether the fruit can only be eaten after it is cooked. Since many of the seeds are inedible, avoid them all to be on the safe side.

The Supermarkets

Be sure to shop in the large modern supermarkets, or *supermercados*. They are a great place to hunt for delicious fruit pastes, unusual spices and lots of freshly roasted cashews and Brazil nuts at very affordable prices. You can also get the makings for a tasty picnic featuring Brazilian food. There are many tempting varieties of cold cuts, sausages and cheeses, many of them regional specialties, at the meat counter. Some cheeses to look for are *queijo de minas,* a cheese similar to muenster, made in the state of Minas Gerais, and *queijo de sertão,* a dry cheese made in the northeastern interior. Don't forget to include some cans of the enormously popular soft drink called *guaraná,* made from the fruit of the same name. And for convenience, before leaving home, pack some tableware and a pocket knife!

Meat and cheese are sold by weight, measured in kilograms (kg). It will be helpful to know how to ask for portions weighing less than a kilogram since a kilogram is equivalent to about 2.2 pounds. I ask for an item by name (or simply point to it, if unlabelled) and then say in Portuguese what part of a kilogram I want.

The following abbreviated list of fractions of a kilogram in Portuguese has proven sufficient to get the quantity I wanted. Corresponding approximate weights in pounds are included.

⅛ (kg): *um oitavo*	~	⅓ pound
¼ (kg): *um quarto*	~	½ pound
⅓ (kg): *um terço*	~	¾ pound
½ (kg): *uma metade*	~	1 pound
¾ (kg): *tres quartos*	~	1½ pound

If you are considering bringing food back to the United States, obtain the Customs and Border Protection (CBP) brochure "Know Before You Go" to find out which agricultural items are allowed. The information is available online as a pdf file at http://www.cbp.gov/xp/cgov/travel/vacation/kbyg. You can also obtain a brochure by calling 1-877-CBP-5511. Listen to the menu and choose the option for ordering brochures. Be aware that websites do change, so you may have to go to the CBP homepage and click on "travel" to get to the webpage of interest if it has changed from the above.

Resources

Mail-Order and Internet Suppliers of Brazilian Food Items

Some retail sources sell the special Brazilian ingredients required for the recipes in this book. These ingredients can be found in Latino and Asian food stores in metropolitan areas and in university towns with large foreign student populations. *Dendê* palm oil, frozen sweet manioc tubers and various manioc flours or meals, such as *farinha de mandioca* and tapioca, usually can be found.

Brazilian food items also can be purchased online from several websites. Since websites change their addresses or URLs and may not be updated regularly, you will probably need to do additional browsing. I suggest that you use your favorite search engine (my standby is google.com) and do a general search for Brazilian food markets or a specific search for a desired ingredient. I hope the following online businesses continue to offer fine Brazilian products for my readers. Please let me know if you discover that any of these sources has gone out of business since this book was printed.

Stores that also have their Brazilian specialty items available for ordering online include:

Pepe's #2 Brasilian Food and Liquor
2333 N. Western Avenue
Chicago, IL 60647
Tel. 773-278-8756
Fax 773-278-8865
shidana69@yahoo.com
http://brasilonline.tripod.com

Supermercado Brazil
10826 Venice Blvd., Ste. 105
Culver City, CA 90232
Tel. 310-837-4299/4297
Fax 310-837-4294
sales@brazilexplore.com
http://www.BrazilianShop.com

Amigofoods.com
7501 NE 3rd Place
Miami FL 33138
Tel. 800-627-2544
Fax: 516-627-0803
customerservice@amigofoods.com
http://www.amigofoods.com

A source for *malagueta* chile pepper seeds to grow in the garden is:

Enchanted Seeds
140 Haasville Rd.
Anthony, NM 88021
Tel. 505-571-2247
http://www.enchantedseeds.com

The website that should be your first choice for up to date information on Brazil (travel, culture, history and nature) is BrazilMax, the hip guide to Brazil. The founding editor, Bill Hinchberger, is an American ex-patriot with an MA degree in Latin American Studies from University of California-Berkeley. Just about everything you need to know to plan your trip is in the section BrazilTravel: A User's Manual to BrazilMax.

hinchber@amcham.com.br
http://www.brazilmax.com

Some Useful Organizations to Know About

Consulate General of Brazil in New York

1185 Avenue of the Americas
21st Floor
New York, NY 10036-2601
Tel: 917-777-7777
Fax: 212-827-0225
consulado@brazilny.org

The Brazilian American Cultural Center

This organization serves as a tourist bureau, providing its members assistance in planning trips to Brazil and discounts on flights. It also helps obtain tourist visas through the Brazilian Consulate in New York. Annual memberships cost $20 and include a monthly newsletter, *The Brazilians,* which contains articles about Brazil and the Brazilian community in the United States.

For more information on joining the Brazilian American Cultural Center, write or call:

The Brazilian American Cultural Center
16 W 46th Street, 2nd Floor
New York, NY 10036
Tel. 212-730-1010
Tel. 800-222-2746

International Organizations

I am a supporter of two international organizations that promote good will and understanding between people of different cultures. These organizations, Servas and The Friendship Force, share similar ideals but operate somewhat differently.

Servas

Servas, from the Esperanto word meaning "serve," is a non-profit system of travelers and hosts. Servas members travel independently and make their own contacts with fellow members in other countries, choosing hosts with attributes of interest from membership rosters. It is a wonderful way to get to know people, be invited into their homes as a family member, share experiences and help promote world peace. As this book was going to press, Servas was negotiating a new location for the organization. Visit their website to find current contact information and to learn more about membership in the organization.

US Servas Committee, Inc.
info@usservas.org
http://www.usservas.org

The Friendship Force

The Friendship Force is a non-profit organization that also fosters good will through encounters between people of different backgrounds. Unlike Servas, Friendship Force members travel in groups to host countries. Both itinerary and travel arrangements are made by a member acting as exchange director. These trips combine stays with a host family and group travel within the host country. For more information on membership in The Friendship Force, write:

The Friendship Force
34 Peachtree St., Suite 900
Atlanta, GA 30303
Tel: 404-522-9490
Fax: 404-688-6148
info@friendshipforce.org
http://www.friendshipforce.org

Helpful Phrases

For Use in Restaurants and Food Markets

In the Restaurant

The following phrases in Portuguese will assist you in ordering food, learning more about the dish you ordered, and determining what specialties of the region are available. Each phrase also is written phonetically to help with pronunciation. Syllables in capital letters are accented. Words or syllables followed by an (ng) have nasal sounds, made by exhaling air through both the nose and mouth when speaking.

MAY I HAVE THE MENU, PLEASE?

Pode trazer-me o cardápio, por favor?
POH-jay trah-ZAY-me oh car-DAH-pee-oh, pour fah-VOAR?

WHAT ARE YOUR "SPECIALS" FOR TODAY?

Qual é o prato do dia?
Kwahl eh oh PRAH-too doh JEE-ah?

DO YOU HAVE . . . ?
(ADD AN ITEM FROM THE MENU GUIDE OR FOODS & FLAVORS GUIDE.)

Vocês tem . . . ?
Voh-SAY-ESE tay(ng) . . . ?

DO YOU HAVE ANY SPECIAL REGIONAL DISHES?

Vocês tem algum prato regional especial?
Voh-SAY-ESE tay(ng) all-GOO(NG) PRAH-too hay-jee-oh-NOW ace-peh-SEE-OW?

WHAT DO YOU RECOMMEND?

O que me recomenda?
Oh kay may he-koh-MAY(NG)-dah?

DO YOU HAVE ANY SPECIAL
FRUITS OR VEGETABLES GROWN
LOCALLY?

Vocé tem alguma fruta ou vegetal
especial plantado nesta região?
*Voh-SAY tay(ng) all-GOO(NG)-ah FRUIT-ah oh vege-jeh-TAU ace-peh-SEE-OW
PLAH(NG)-tah-doh NEHS-tah
heh-JEE-OW?*

WHAT FRESH TROPICAL FRUITS OR
FRUIT JUICES DO YOU HAVE?

Quais frutas tropicais ou sucos de
frutas tropicais você tem?
*Koo-EYE-ESE FRUIT-as troh-pee-KAH-ese
oh SUE-kohs jee troh-pee-KAH-ese
voh-SAY tay(ng)?*

I WOULD LIKE (SOME) . . .

Queria . . .
Ker-RE-a . . .

I/WE WOULD LIKE TO ORDER . . .

Eu/nos gostaria/gostariamos de
pedir . . .
Ah-oh/naws goh-stah-REE-ah/goh-stah-REE-ah-mohs jee pee-DJEAR . . .

WHAT ARE THE INGREDIENTS IN
THIS DISH?

Quais são os ingredientes neste prato?
Koo-EYE-ESE sow ohs een-gray-jee-ay(ng)-CHEES NEHST-chee PRAH-too?

WHAT ARE THE FLAVORINGS/
SEASONINGS IN THIS DISH?

Quais são os temperos neste prato?
*Koo-EYE-ESE sow ohs tay(ng)-pay-ROHS
NEHST-chee prah-too?*

IS THIS DISH SPICY?

Este prato é apimentado?
*AYSH-chee PRAH-too eh
ah-pee-may(ng)-TAH-doh?*

In the Market

The following phrases will help you make purchases and learn more about unfamiliar produce.

WHAT IS THIS?

O que é isto?
Oh kay eh ESE-toh?

WHAT IS THIS CALLED?

Como se chama isto?
COH-moo say SHAH-mah ESE-toh?

WHAT IS THE NAME OF THIS FRUIT/VEGETABLE?

Qual é o nome desta fruta/deste vegetal?
Kwahl eh oh NOH-me DAS-stah FRUIT-a/DEH-stay vege-jeh-TAU?

DO YOU HAVE . . . ?
(ADD AN ITEM FROM THE *FOODS & FLAVORS guide*)

Você tem . . . ?
Voh-SAY tay(ng) . . . ?

MAY I TASTE THIS?

Posso provar isto?
POH-sue proh-VAHR ESE-toh?

WHERE CAN I BUY . . . ?

Onde é que eu posso comprar . . . ?
AW(NG)-jee eh kay ah-oh POH-sue caw(ng)-PRARE . . . ?

HOW MUCH IS THIS PER KILO-GRAM/LOTE?

Quanto custa isto por kilo/lote?
KWAH(NG)-TOO COOSH-tah ESE-toh pour KEY-loh/LOH-chee?

I WOULD LIKE TO BUY . . . KILOGRAMS OF THIS/THAT.

Eu gostaria de comprar kilos disto/daquilo.
Ah-oh goh-stah-REE-ah jee caw(ng)-PRARE KEY-lohs jees-toh/dah-KEY-loh.

67

HELPFUL PHRASES

Other Useful Phrases

Sometimes it helps to see in writing a word or phrase that is said to you in Portuguese, because certain combinations of letters have distinctly different sounds in Portuguese than in English. You may be familiar with the word and its English translation but less familiar with its pronunciation. The following phrase comes in handy if you want to see the word or phrase you are hearing:

PLEASE WRITE IT ON THIS PIECE OF PAPER.

Por favor, escreva nesse papel.
Pour fah-VOAR ese-CRAY-vah NAY-see pah-PE-HOH.

Interested in bringing home books about Brazilian food? Perhaps some restaurateurs know just the place for you to look if you pose the following questions:

WHERE CAN I BUY A BRAZILIAN COOKBOOK IN ENGLISH?

Onde eu posso comprar um livro de culinária brasileira em inglês?
AW(NG)-jee ah-oh POH-sue caw(ng)-PRARE oo(ng) LEE-vro jee coo-lee-NAH-ree-ah bra-zee-LAY-rah ay(ng) ee(ng)-GLAYSH?

WHERE CAN I BUY A BOOK ABOUT BRAZILIAN FOOD IN ENGLISH?

Onde eu posso comprar um livro sobre comida brasileira em inglês?
AW(NG)-jee ah-oh POH-sue caw(ng)-PRARE oo(ng) LEE-vro soh-bre coh-ME-dah bra-zee-LAY-rah ay(ng) ee(ng)-GLAYSH?

And, of course, the following phrases also are handy to know:

IS SMOKING PERMITTED?

É permitido fumar?
Eh pehr-me-CHEE-doh foo-MAHR?

68

WHERE IS THE LADIES'/MENS' RESTROOM?

Onde é o banheiro dos mulheres/homens?

AW(NG)-jee eh oh bah-KNEE-YEAH-roh dohs moo-LEE-AY-rese/OH-mien?

THE CHECK PLEASE.

A conta por favor.

Ah CAW(NG)-tah pour fah-VOAR.

DO YOU ACCEPT CREDIT CARDS? TRAVELERS CHECKS?

Vocês aceitam cartão de credito? Travelers checks?

Voh-SAY-ESE ah-SAY-tah(ng) car-TAU jee CRAH-jee-toh? TRAH-vel-ors checks?

THANK YOU VERY MUCH.
THE FOOD WAS DELICIOUS.
("Thank-you" is based on the gender of the speaker.
Women say obrigada; men, obrigado.)

Muito obrigado/a. A comida estava deliciosa.

MOY-EE-toh oh-bree-GAH-doo/dah. Ah koh-MEE-dah es-TAH-vah day-LEE-SI-OH-zah.

Menu Guide

This alphabetical listing is an extensive compilation of menu entries in Portuguese, with English translations, to make ordering food easy. It includes typical Brazilian fare as well as specialties characteristic of each of the five regions of Brazil: the north, northeast, center-west, southeast and south.

Classic regional dishes of Brazil that should not be missed are labeled "regional classic" in the margin next to the menu entry. Note that outside a particular geographical area, these specialties rarely are available unless a restaurant features one or more regional cuisines. Some noteworthy dishes popular throughout the country—also not to be missed—are labeled "national favorite." Comments on some of our favorites also are included in the margin.

With *Eat Smart in Brazil* in hand, you will quickly become more familiar with restaurant cuisine. Also have it with you at breakfast in the hotel; there will be plenty of items to identify. While Brazilians eat a light breakfast, the customary complimentary one in hotels often is an elaborate spread—several varieties of fruits and fruit juices, cheeses, breads, cereals, cakes, eggs and meat await you. Even the smaller establishments provide an adequate selection.

In restaurants, breakfast, or *café da manha,* generally is served 7–10 AM. The main meal of the day is lunch, or *almoço,* which is served from about 11:30 AM–3 PM. Dinner, or *jantar,* is served from 7–11 PM. In metropolitan areas Brazilians dine late. If you arrive much before 10 PM on the weekends, you'll probably be in the company of other tourists.

abacaxi assado baked pineapple.

abacaxi com côco pineapple with coconut.

abacaxi com vinho fresh pineapple sprinkled with sugar and doused with claret.

abará small bean cakes made of mashed brown beans or black-eyed peas, smoked shrimp, ginger and ground *malagueta* peppers and steamed in banana leaves.   REGIONAL CLASSIC

abóbora refogada stewed pumpkin seasoned with scallions and garlic.

abobrinha frita fried squash.

acacá a confection of boiled, fermented hominy corn made into balls, rolled in banana leaves and served chilled.

REGIONAL CLASSIC **acarajé** fritters made from a batter of skinned, puréed beige beans, ground dried shrimp, ginger and onion. They are fried in *dendê* palm oil and typically embellished with a stuffing of *vatapá,* a purée of dried shrimp, cashews, peanuts, bread and coconut milk or with *molho de acarajé,* a sauce of shrimp, dried *malagueta peppers,* cilantro and ginger.

afogado de carangueijo boiled whole crab.

REFRESHING **agua de côco** coconut water served fresh in the coconut.

agulhas fritas fried needlefish.

NATIONAL FAVORITE **aipim frito** fried pieces of manioc.

alcatra à jardineira round steak garnished with a variety of cooked vegetables.

alfenins de côco "melt-away" candies made with coconut milk.

almôndegas meatballs.

DELICIOUS **ambrosia** a dessert made of milk, sugar syrup and egg yolks, simmered until thickened and browned, seasoned with cloves and cinnamon.

NATIONAL FAVORITE **amor em pedaços (love in pieces)** bars made with sugar cookie dough topped with merengue and almonds. They are cut into squares or broken into small pieces.

angú de arroz a molded porridge of rice and coconut milk.

REGIONAL CLASSIC **angú de milho** a molded porridge of corn meal cooked in salted water.

arabú a dish made from a mixture of flour and the yolk of turtle eggs (an endangered species).

arroz à grega rice mixed with small pieces of carrot, bacon, and raisins and flavored with a touch of vinegar.

NATIONAL FAVORITE **arroz brasileiro** rice briefly fried in oil, onion and garlic before boiling.

arroz carioca rice cooked with chicken, bacon, pork sausages and tomatoes.

arroz com camarões rice with shrimp.

arroz com guariroba rice with hearts of *guariroba* palm.

arroz com leite de côco rice with coconut milk.

arroz com mariscos rice with shellfish.

arroz com porco rice covered with sautéed cubes of pork seasoned with garlic, *malagueta* peppers and cilantro.

arroz com suã rice cooked with the meat from neck bones.

arroz de carreteiro (wagoner's rice) rice with rehydrated, REGIONAL CLASSIC sun-dried beef, tomato, green pepper, onion and *malagueta* peppers.

arroz de cuxá a rice and vegetable dish seasoned with the young leaves and sesame-like seeds of the red sorrel plant, or *vinegreira*.

arroz de haussa (arroz de haucá; arroz d'aussa) com carne picada rice topped with pieces of sun-dried beef, sautéed in onions and garlic. (Many of the slaves in Brazil were members of the Haussa tribe in Africa.)

arroz de viúva (widow's rice) rice cooked in thin coconut milk.

arroz doce a sweet rice pudding, often topped with caramelized NATIONAL FAVORITE sugar or cinnamon.

arroz simples plain rice.

azeitonas recheadas com filés de enchovas pitted olives stuffed with a paste of anchovies flavored with lemon juice.

azeitonas temperadas olives marinated in olive oil with oregano SPICY and *malagueta* peppers.

baba de macã a cake topped with a jelly-like apple mixture.

baba de moça (maiden's drool) a mixture of sugar syrup, egg NATIONAL FAVORITE yolks and coconut milk, sprinkled with cinnamon.

bacalhau à brás a mixture of shredded salted codfish, eggs and lightly fried, home-style shoestring potatoes.

bacalhau à gomes de sá salted codfish, sliced potatoes, onions, TASTY and black olives, garnished with quartered hard-boiled eggs.

bacalhau à mineira salted codfish with shredded kale.

bacalhau à portuguesa salted codfish placed between alternating NATIONAL FAVORITE layers of sliced tomatoes and potatoes, and baked.

bacalhau assado baked salted codfish topped with oil and red wine vinegar just before serving.

bacalhau brasileiro salted fish, of a local variety, not salted codfish (*bacalhau*) imported from Portugal.

bacalhau com leite do côco salted codfish in coconut milk.

bacalhau em molho salted codfish in a tomato-based sauce containing beaten egg yolks.

bacalhoada see *bacalhau à portuguesa.*

badejo assado no vapor com molho de pimentão baked and steamed sea bass with a green pepper sauce.

REGIONAL CLASSIC **baião de dois** white rice and navy beans cooked together with onions, coconut milk and sun-dried meat and topped with melted goat cheese.

DELICIOUS **bamba de couve** corn porridge with shredded kale and pieces of pork loin.

banana assada com queijo bananas covered with cheese, cinnamon and sugar, and baked.

banana-da-terra frita fried, unripe plantain.

REGIONAL CLASSIC **barreado** a stew of beef, salt pork and herbs, traditionally cooked slowly in a clay pot.

batata corada small boiled potatoes fried in seasoned butter. Also called *batata cozida.*

batata cozida see *batata corada.*

batata cozida com pele boiled, unpeeled potatoes.

batata doce assada roasted sweet potatoes.

batata doce frita fried sweet potatoes.

batata nozete ball-shaped pieces of potato sautéed in butter.

TASTY **batata palha** deep-fried shredded potatoes. Also called *batata palita.*

batata palita see *batata palha.*

NATIONAL FAVORITE **batida** a drink of fresh fruit juice and *cachaça,* the Brazilian brandy made from sugar cane.

batida de amendoim a drink consisting of ground peanuts, sweetened condensed milk and *cachaça,* the Brazilian brandy made from sugar cane.

batida de jabuticaba a drink containing juice from the *jabuticaba* fruit and *cachaça*, the Brazilian brandy made from sugar cane.

batida paulista a drink of lemon juice, egg white and *cachaça,* the Brazilian brandy made from sugar cane, served in a glass with sugar on the rim.

baurú a club sandwich of ham or bacon, fried egg, cheese, lettuce and tomato.

SCRUMPTIOUS **beijinhos de côco** little candy kisses made of grated coconut and sweetened condensed milk.

beijinhos de moça (maiden's kisses) small candies made from coconut, egg yolks and grated cheese.

beijos de anjo (angel kisses) sweets made of eggs and sugar, simmered and served in sugar syrup flavored with vanilla and cloves.

beijos de cabocla (farmer's daughter's kisses) coconut kisses.

beijos de mamão papaya kisses.

beijú an appetizer made of fried tapioca, often sprinkled with coconut, and formed into pancakes or into thin, crisp finger-length strips. This appetizer is also called *tapioca*, or *tapioca com côco*, when topped with coconut.   REGIONAL CLASSIC

bem casados (well-married) wedding cookies made from eggs, sugar and potato starch. Two cookies are bonded together with a filling.   NATIONAL FAVORITE

beringela (berinjela) com tomates baked eggplant and tomatoes.

bife à cavalo steak topped with a fried egg.   DELICIOUS

bife de fígado acebolado beef liver with onions.

bifes com cerveja sirloin steak cooked in beer.

bifes de lagarto com molho picante round steak with hot sauce.

bifes de tênder com ameixas e damascos ham steaks with prunes and apricots.   EXCELLENT CHOICE

bifes enrolados thin steaks rolled around various fillings such as carrot strips, bacon or green pepper.

biscoitos de côco coconut cookies.

biscoitos de maisena cornstarch cookies.

biscoitos de nozes nut cookies.

biscoitos de sal salt crackers.

biscoitos lingua de gato (cat's tongue cookies) ribbon-shaped sugar cookies.

bobó de camarão fresh shrimp in a purée of dried shrimp, manioc meal, coconut milk, cashews and peanuts, flavored with *dendê* palm oil.   REGIONAL CLASSIC

bobó de inhame puréed yam mixed with ground shrimp, onion, garlic, ginger and *malagueta* peppers, stir-fried in *dendê* palm oil.

boca de carangueijo the large, anterior pair of crab legs sautéed in butter.   NOT TO BE MISSED

bode assado com farofa de água fria roasted goat meat with browned, coarsely ground manioc meal.

bolinhos de amêndoa almond candy balls.

bolinhos de arroz deep-fried balls made of cooked rice mixed with egg and seasonings.

bolinhos de peixe deep-fried balls made of shredded fried fish, seasonings and egg.

NATIONAL FAVORITE **bolinhos de queijo** deep-fried balls made of grated cheese mixed with whipped egg white and dipped in flour.

bolinhos estudantes small, sweet balls of fried manioc meal and coconut.

bôlo com amendoas almond cake.

bôlo comum plain cake.

SUPER **bôlo de aipim** a moist cake made with manioc meal and grated coconut. Also called *bôlo de macaxeira*.

bôlo de carioca a lemon spice cake with molasses and stout.

bôlo de cerveja a cake made with beer.

NATIONAL FAVORITE **bôlo de fubá e cajú** a cake of cornmeal and cashews.

bôlo de legumes a vegetable cake.

bôlo de macaxeira see *bôlo de aipim*.

bôlo de vitela veal loaf.

bôlo diamantina a yeast cake with cooked potato and pumpkin, molasses, and anise seed flavoring.

bôlo espera marido ('hoping for a husband' cake) a rich, white layer cake with coconut milk and freshly grated coconut.

TASTY **bôlo frio de bacalhau e enchovas** a chilled, molded mayonnaise-based "cake" of mashed codfish, anchovies, potatoes and seasonings.

bôlo inglês a cake with candied fruit.

REMARKABLE **bôlo para agradar as sogras (cake to please mothers-in-law)** a raisin cake flavored with orange and lemon rind.

bôlo para vinho a cake flavored with orange rind and cinnamon, toasted and eaten with wine.

bôlo quero mais ('I want more' cake) a sheet spice cake made with candied fruits, yogurt, nutmeg, cinnamon and cloves.

bombocado a pudding-like concoction made from coconut milk, egg yolks, sugar, grated coconut and cheese.

bombom de castanha do pará a Brazil nut bonbon.

NATIONAL FAVORITE **bombom de uva** a bonbon consisting of a fresh grape surrounded by a rich sugar-and-egg mixture.

braço com repôlho agridoce beef arm roast with sweet–sour red cabbage.

braseiro de frutos do mar fish and seafood grilled over a brazier.

brasileiras Brazilian coconut cookies.

NATIONAL FAVORITE **brigadeiros** a rich chocolate dessert made with condensed milk.

broa de milho corn bread.

brochete de filé à campanha beef steak on a skewer, country style.

buchada de carneiro mutton tripe. REGIONAL CLASSIC

cabrito assado roasted goat (kid).

caçarola de milho com camarão corn and shrimp casserole.

cachaça Brazilian brandy made from sugar cane. POTENT

cachimbo a drink consisting of honey, lime juice and *cachaça,* the Brazilian brandy made from sugar cane, served warm.

café com leite coffee with hot milk.

café sem açúcar black, unsweetened coffee.

cafezinho strong coffee with sugar, served in demitasse. NATIONAL FAVORITE

cafezinho carioca coffee with sugar served in demitasse. It is diluted with hot water and is weaker than regular *cafezinho.*

caipirinha a drink of crushed lemon, sugar and *cachaça,* the NATIONAL FAVORITE Brazilian brandy made from sugar cane.

caipiríssima a drink of white rum and crushed lemon.

caipiroska a drink of vodka and crushed lemon.

cajuzinho a sweet made of ground peanuts, cocoa and eggs, TASTY rolled in sugar.

calabresa na chapa grilled sausage.

calda de ameixa prune syrup.

caldeirada de pescador a hearty stew made with fresh fish and MILD & FLAVORFUL vegetables.

caldeirada de tambaquí *tambaquí* fish stew.

caldeirada de tucunaré *tucunaré* fish stew.

caldinho de peixe a small cup of fish soup.

caldo broth made from soup bones.

caldo de cana freshly squeezed juice from sugar cane. NATIONAL FAVORITE

caldo verde a potato-based soup with shredded kale and sausage, flavored with cilantro, onion and garlic.

camarão alho e óleo garlic shrimp.

camarão cozido na casca cooked, unshelled shrimp.

camarões à baiana e quiabo shrimp and okra in coconut milk thickened with manioc meal.

camarões à paulista unshelled shrimp marinated in lemon juice REGIONAL CLASSIC and cilantro, and fried in olive oil and garlic.

camarões aferventados com molho tártaro boiled shrimp with tartar sauce.

EXCELLENT CHOICE **camarões casadinhos** (married shrimp) two large shrimp, split and stuffed with manioc meal, placed side by side, two to a skewer, and grilled. Also called *casadinhos de camarão.*

camarões e ostras com macarrão shrimp and oysters with macaroni.

NATIONAL FAVORITE **camarões empanados** shrimp fried in batter.

camarões torrados em casca shrimp browned in the shell.

canapés de presunto e aspargo smoked ham and asparagus canapés.

canapés de salmão salmon canapés.

NATIONAL FAVORITE **canja** Brazilian-style chicken soup containing pieces of boiled chicken and rice in a seasoned chicken broth. Also called *canja de galinha.*

canja de galinha see *canja.*

NATIONAL FAVORITE **canjica** a dessert of white hominy corn or grated sweet corn, coconut milk, sweetened condensed milk and peanuts, sprinkled with cinnamon or cloves. Also called *mugunzá,* or *mungunzá,* in the north and northeast.

canudinho an appetizer consisting of a hollow cylinder of dough stuffed with various fillings.

capim limão lemon grass tea.

caramela a custard with caramelized sugar.

NOT TO BE MISSED **carangueijo à marajoara** crabmeat in a sauce of coconut, tomatoes, onion and oregano, in the style of Marajó Island.

carangueijo mole soft-shelled crab cooked in a spicy sauce.

carangueijo refogado crab stewed in a seasoned broth.

carangueijos recheados com ovos duros e azeitonas crab shells stuffed with a crabmeat mixture containing chopped hard-boiled eggs and olives, topped with buttered bread crumbs and browned in the oven.

carimã a sun-dried cake of manioc meal.

DELICIOUS **carne assada ao molho ferrugem** roast beef in a brown sauce derived from the meat juices.

carne de panela pot roast.

NATIONAL FAVORITE **carne de sol na manteiga de garrafa** salted, sun-dried meat with clarified butter.

carne ensopada na cerveja beef stewed in beer.

carne picadinha a stew of coarsely chopped beef or pork.

carne seca com abóbora dried beef with pumpkin.

carne seca frita fried sun-dried meat.

carpaccio paper-thin slices of raw sirloin or filet mignon drizzled   EXCELLENT CHOICE
with a sauce of lemon juice, olive oil and capers.

carrê de cordeiro loin of lamb.

cartola a banana baked with cheese, cinnamon and sugar.

carurú okra cooked with ground, dried smoked shrimp, ground   NATIONAL FAVORITE
peanuts and cashews, *malagueta* peppers and cilantro in *dendê*
palm oil.

casadinhos de camarão see *camarões casadinhos.*

casquinha de lagosta cooked lobster, meat seasoned with fried
garlic and onions and returned to an empty lobster tail,
sprinkled with toasted manioc meal and baked.

casquinho de carangueijo cooked crab meat with coconut milk,   FABULOUS
tomatoes, *malagueta* peppers, onion and cilantro. The mixture
is stuffed into an empty crab shell, sprinkled with grated cheese
or manioc meal and baked.

cavaquinha ao molho de manteiga a small lobster served with
melted butter.

cebolas brancas no vinagre shallots pickled in red wine vinegar
with garlic, lemon and peppercorns.

cenouras ensopadas stewed carrots.

chambaril com pirão beef hocks or shanks with creamed manioc.   MILD & FLAVORFUL

charutos cabbage leaves rolled and shaped into "cigars" and
steamed.

chibé a beverage made by adding *cachaça,* the Brazilian brandy
made from sugar cane, to the drink known as *jacúba,* which
consists of manioc meal and water, sweetened with sugar or
honey.

chocolate quente hot chocolate.

chouriço e brócolos com creme de milho smoked pork sausage
and broccoli with creamed corn.

chuchu com camarão green squash with shrimp. Also called   TASTY
xuxu com camarão.

chucrute com paio sauerkraut with pork sausage.

churrasco the *gaúcho* (cowboy) style, hearty Brazilian barbecue   NATIONAL FAVORITE
featuring an abundance of meats and sausages grilled on skewers
or on a spit.

cocada white coconut candy. The dark-brown version contains
burned brown sugar.

cocada branca a compote (white) of sugar, cloves, milk and grated coconut.

DELICIOUS **cocada com abóbora** a compote of cooked pumpkin, cloves, sugar and grated coconut.

cocada preta a compote (dark) of brown sugar, cinnamon, cloves and grated coconut.

NATIONAL FAVORITE **côco gelado** chilled coconut water.

côco loco a dessert of coconut and chocolate.

coelho baiano braised rabbit with orange and lemon juice, green peppers and mushrooms.

cogumelos recheados stuffed mushrooms.

NATIONAL FAVORITE **compota de frutas** fruit compote.

compota de manga mango compote.

compota de maracujá passion fruit compote.

compote de ameixas compote of prunes cooked in vanilla, lemon and sugar.

contrafilé à milanesa breaded sirloin.

coquetel de camarão shrimp cocktail.

coquetel de lagosta lobster cocktail.

coracões de frango no espeto chicken hearts grilled on a skewer.

coração recheado stuffed beef heart.

corvinas grelhadas grilled croaker fish.

EXCELLENT CHOICE **costelas bovinas com arroz de açafrão** beef ribs with saffron rice.

costelas de tambaquí na brasa com manteiga e limão "rib steaks" of *tambaquí* fish grilled with butter and lemon.

NATIONAL FAVORITE **costeletas de porco** pork chops.

costelinha stewed ham ribs.

REGIONAL CLASSIC **couve à mineira** shredded kale sautéed briefly in oil, onion and garlic.

couve flor de panela pan-cooked cauliflower.

coxas apimentadas chicken legs broiled in hot pepper sauce.

coxas de frango chicken legs.

coxas de rã frog legs.

NATIONAL FAVORITE **coxinha** an appetizer of breaded "mock" chicken legs or a pastry filled with chicken. A filling other than chicken will be specified.

coxinha de catupiri an appetizer of pastry filled with *catupiri* cheese.

NATIONAL FAVORITE **cozido à brasileira** Brazilian-style stew. This bountiful dish contains many different meats and vegetables including beef,

TOP *Camarão na moranga,* a tasty main dish of winter squash filled with a creamy shrimp mixture. The shrimp are flamed in cognac for added flavor. **MIDDLE** Heavenly dessert treats called *quindins de yá-yá.* These small treasures, made of sugar, egg yolks and coconut, are to die for! **BOTTOM** Popular appetizers, or *salgadinhos,* called *coxinhas.* They typically are filled with a chicken mixture.

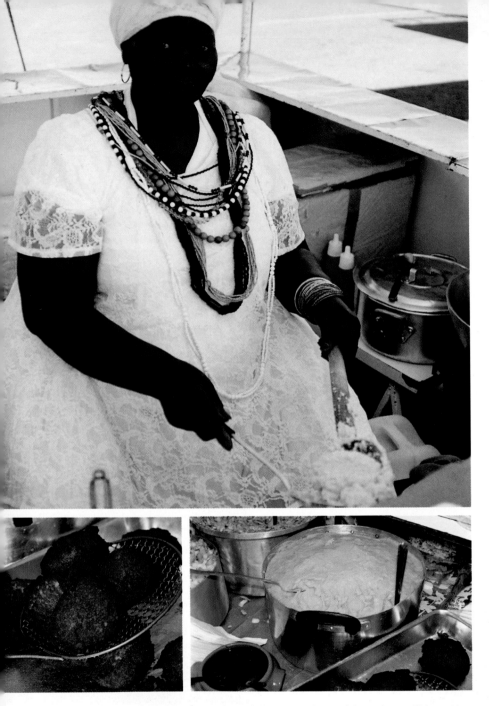

TOP A *Baiana* in her outdoor stall, preparing batter for the famous fritters of the northeast called *acarajé,* which are made of skinned, puréed beige beans, dried shrimp, ginger and onion. **ABOVE LEFT** *Acarajé* fried in *dendê* palm oil. Follow the scent of *dendê* oil sputtering in large pots to locate this popular and traditional street food. **ABOVE RIGHT** Delicious embellishments for *acarajé,* including yellow-colored *vatapá,* a purée of dried shrimp, cashews, peanuts, bread and coconut milk.

TOP "Braguinha," the singing breakfast chef at the Petribu Sheraton in Recife. His specialty is a thin pancake of fried tapioca and grated coconut called *beijú*, or *tapioca com côco*. **MIDDLE** Buying fresh vegetables in the *Ver-O-Peso* market on the waterfront in Belém. A sampler of sliced vegetables atop large leaves and bundles of *chuchu*, a small, light-green squash, are visible in the foreground. **BOTTOM** Fruit in the *Ver-O-Peso* market in Belém. In baskets in the foreground, green lemons, *pupunha* still on the stem, and *bacuri* tempt the passerby. Loose on the wooden pallet are large *cupuaçu* fruits, whose pulp is sweet and delicious.

TOP A sweet seller in Brasília. Deep kettles hold rich treats (*doces*) made of fruit or coconut sweetened with sugar. Nearby are tempting red bricks of guava paste, or *goiabada,* and tan blocks of a milk pudding thick enough to cut, called *doce de leite de cortar.* Also for sale, either fresh (in plastic) or aged, is the popular cheese made in Minas Gerais, called *queijo de minas.* **ABOVE LEFT** *Doce de leite,* a rich, soft caramel mixture made from thickened milk and sugar. **ABOVE RIGHT** *Doce de figo,* figs stewed in thick sugar syrup.

TOP LEFT A young man in the *Ver-O-Peso* market in Belém grinding manioc leaves (*maniva*). The ground leaves are a key ingredient for some traditional dishes of the north such as *maniçoba,* a meat and giblet stew. **MIDDLE** Baskets of sweet manioc tubers in the *Ver-O-Peso* waterfront market in Belém. This variety of manioc tuber is called *aipim, macaxeira* and *mandioca doce,* meaning sweet manioc. The tubers are pared, boiled or fried, and eaten like potatoes. **BOTTOM** Sacks of manioc flour in the *Ver-O-Peso* market in Belém. This meal, available in several grades of coarseness, is made from pulp of the poisonous variety of manioc tubers after it has been detoxified.

TOP Rows of luscious *mamão,* a larger and somewhat less sweet version of papaya. Generous wedges of *mamão,* the inner surface studded with round, black seeds, typically are served for breakfast. **ABOVE LEFT** Stacks of the elongated *abóbora,* a member of the pumpkin family. It is usually sold by the chunk. **ABOVE RIGHT** *Jilo,* a small, green vegetable belonging to the deadly nightshade family. Owing to its bitterness, it is often called *jilo amargo,* meaning "bitter" *jilo.*

TOP LEFT Crates of the sugar apple fruit in an outdoor market in Rio. This fruit, known as *ata, fruto do conde* and *pinha,* has pulp with a scrumptious pear-like taste. **TOP RIGHT** The Chinese persimmon, or *kaki,* a soft fruit popular in the outdoor markets. It looks like a tomato and has a pleasant, sweet taste. **ABOVE** A potpourri of fruit in an outdoor market in Brasília. The yellow, uneven-surfaced fruit in the foreground is the tangy wild tangerine, or *mexerica.*

TOP LEFT Making *caldo do cana,* or sugar cane juice, in Brasília. Watching the clattering machinery grind up stalks of cane is fascinating. **TOP RIGHT** A young man in the *Ver-O-Peso* market in Belém cutting a block of *charque ponta de agulha,* the sun-dried meat made from a cut of beef called *ponta de agulha,* which is similar to beef brisket. **ABOVE** A fishmonger in the *Mercado Municipal* in Manaus, an ornate ironwork structure at the waterfront that serves as a food market. The fine *tambaquí* fish he holds is a fruit- and seed-eating fish with powerful, molar-like teeth adapted for crushing food.

pork, *lingüiça* sausage, sweet potatoes, winter squash, plantains, sweet manioc and chunks of corn on the cob.

cozido de peito com aipim e repôlho a stew of beef brisket with pieces of manioc and cabbage.

creme de abacate a dessert or thick beverage made with avocado, milk and sugar.

creme de abóboras com toucinho cream of pumpkin with bacon.

creme de arroz a creamed mixture of rice, rice flour, milk and coconut milk.   TASTY

creme de côco a coconut pudding made with coconut milk thickened with cornstarch.

creme de ostras com palmito oysters in a white sauce with shredded palm hearts.

creme de palmito a creamy soup with hearts of palm.

creme do céu baked orange-flavored custard.

croquettes de camarões shrimp croquettes.   NATIONAL FAVORITE

cuca de mel a honey cake using yeast as leavening agent.

cupim prized fat-marbled meat from the "humpback" of zebu   NATIONAL FAVORITE
(Brahma) steer, a featured item in most *churrascos,* or Brazilian barbecues.

curau sweet or seasoned cornmeal prepared in corn husks.

cuscuz de fubá com camarão a molded corn meal porridge (couscous) with shrimp, coconut and seasonings.

cuscuz de galinha a savory molded corn meal porridge (couscous) with chicken.

cuscuz de tapioca a sweet molded cake made from tapioca,   REGIONAL CLASSIC
sugar, coconut milk and grated coconut. Also known as *tapioca cuscuz.*

cuscuz paulista a savory, molded corn meal porridge (couscous)   REGIONAL CLASSIC
with shrimp, sardines, tomatoes, hearts-of-palm, olives and hard-boiled eggs.

cuxa a dish made of rice and vegetables seasoned with young leaves of the red sorrel shrub, or *vinegreira,* growing in the northeastern region of Brazil. It also can contain the sesame-like seeds from this plant.

delicia an egg and coconut pudding.

delicia de abóbora puréed sweetened pumpkin in coconut milk.

delicias de demasco apricot candies coated with grated coconut.

dobradinha com feijão branco tripe with white beans in a tomato-based sauce.

FABULOUS **doce de abóbora** a compote of puréed sweetened pumpkin, seasoned with sugar, cinnamon and cloves.

doce de arroz rice pudding.

doce de banana em rodinhas poached banana slices in sugar syrup, flavored with cloves and cinnamon.

doce de buriti a paste made from the *buriti* palm fruit.

REGIONAL CLASSIC **doce de cupuaçu** a compote of *cupuaçu* fruit in a heavy syrup.

doce de fruta fruit stewed in a thick syrup. Also called *doce em compota.*

VERY SWEET **doce de leite** a rich, soft caramel mixture made from thickened milk and sugar. It is sometimes put in small pastry shells.

doce em compota see *doce de fruta.*

docinhos de abóbora pumpkin candy.

docinhos de amendoim small candies of ground peanuts, eggs, sugar and coconut.

REGIONAL CLASSIC **efo** pieces of grouper fish in a mixture of dried shrimp paste, steamed red spinach leaves known as beef tongue, or *lingua de vaca,* ground peanuts and coconut milk. It is usually flavored with *dendê* palm oil.

empadão de galinha a large (family-size) empanada filled with chicken.

empadas de carne empanadas filled with a meat mixture.

empadinhas de camarão baked bite-size empanadas filled with shrimp.

NATIONAL FAVORITE **empadinhas de galinha** baked bite-size empanadas filled with chicken.

enchovas a paste of anchovies, *malagueta* peppers, onion, garlic and olive oil.

enguias fritas fried eels.

DELICIOUS **enrolado** a baked finger-length appetizer made by winding a thin strip of dough several times around a filling until it is completely encased.

ensopado de chuchu com camarão stewed squash with shrimp in coconut milk.

ensopado de lagosta marinated lobster stewed in coconut milk.

ensopado de palmito stewed hearts-of-palm in coconut milk.

ensopado de tambaquí stewed *tambaquí* fish in coconut milk.   EXCELLENT CHOICE

ervilhas na manteiga buttered peas.

escabeche de peixe pickled fish.

escalapinho de tucunaré a thin filet of *tucunaré* fish.

escaldado de perú a stew made with pieces of roast turkey, dried beef and vegetables.

esfirra a savory pastry stuffed with spiced meat. The meat is   NATIONAL FAVORITE
placed in the center of a square of dough and covered as the four corners are brought up over it and pinched together in the center.

espetinhos de camarão shrimp marinated in garlic and lemon juice and grilled on small skewers.

espeto misto mixed grill of meat on a skewer.   WONDERFUL

espinafre com manteiga buttered spinach.

espuma de goiaba a frothy dessert of puréed guava in syrup with lemon juice and beaten egg whites.

espumas de côco baianas a fluffy coconut pudding of grated   REFRESHING
coconut and milk, thickened with egg yolk.

farinha na manteiga manioc meal lightly browned in butter.   NATIONAL FAVORITE

farofa amarela manioc meal lightly browned in *dendê* palm oil.

farofa brasileira manioc meal lightly browned in butter with eggs and bacon.

farofa de abóbora manioc meal browned in butter and mixed with chunks of pumpkin.

farofa de banana bananas fried with onion rings and manioc meal.

farofa de ouro manioc meal browned in butter, mixed with chopped, hard-boiled egg yolks and served with egg-white halves filled with olives.

farofa de pirarucú fried manioc meal with shredded *pirarucú* fish and onion.

farofa molhada no côco fried manioc meal moistened with coconut milk.

fatias de côco coconut bars.

feijão de côco puréed black beans in coconut milk, lightly sweetened with sugar and sometimes flavored with *dendê* palm oil.

feijão tropeiro (mule driver's beans) whole, cooked black or   REGIONAL CLASSIC
beige beans sautéed in olive oil, garlic, onion, parsley and

chives, thickened with manioc flour. This bean preparation traditionally is served with eggs, sausages and grilled pork chops (compare with *virado de feijão,* which has the same accompanying items but the beans are mashed, not whole).

A FEAST **feijoada or feijoada completa** the spectacular national dish of Brazil. This is an elaborate stew with black beans and many different smoked and sun-dried meats, especially pork, and smoked sausages. It is served with several traditional side dishes, including orange slices, shredded kale, rice, manioc meal browned in butter *(farofa)* and a hot pepper and lemon sauce called *molho de pimenta e limão.*

fígado acebolado calves' liver with onions.

INTERESTING **figos com presunto** figs with smoked ham.

figos recheados stuffed figs.

filé ao sal grosso steak rubbed with coarse salt before grilling.

filé de surubim filet of *surubim* fish.

GREAT CHOICE **filé medalhão com ervas** filet mignon topped with a lemon slice and a dollop of seasoned butter.

filet de linguado ao molho de camarão filet of sole with shrimp sauce.

NATIONAL FAVORITE **filet grelhado à palito** grilled filet of beef on wooden sticks.

filhote ao leite do côco baked *filhote* fish in coconut milk sauce.

filhote de forno ao queijo do marajó baked *filhote* fish with buffalo cheese from Marajó Island.

SPECTACULAR **fios de ovos** egg threads. This is a spectacular dessert novelty made by pouring egg yolks slowly through a special 3-holed strainer or through small holes in the end of an egg shell into boiling sugar syrup. It is often a topping for other desserts.

folhas verdes green leaf salad.

forminhas de camarão shrimp molds.

forminhas de espinafre spinach molds.

frango à caçador (hunter's chicken) chicken with mashed potatoes, rice and vegetables.

NATIONAL FAVORITE **frango à passarinho ao alho e óleo** small pieces of chicken cooked in garlic and oil.

frango ao molho pardo a chicken stew in sauce containing fresh chicken blood.

frango assado de forno com passas oven-roasted chicken with raisins.

NATIONAL FAVORITE **frango com quiabo** pieces of chicken cooked in broth with chopped okra.

frango com tomates e bananas chicken simmered in white wine and tomatoes and covered with fried bananas.

frango grelhado com creme de milho grilled chicken with creamed corn.

frango na púcara a mixture of chicken, ham, tomatoes and onion in a port wine sauce, baked in a deep earthenware casserole *(púcara)*.

frango no leite chicken cooked in milk.

frango resfriado cold chicken.

frigideira de bacalhau salted codfish baked in a mixture of tomatoes, beaten eggs, cilantro and coconut milk.

frigideira de caranguejo ou camarão crabmeat or shrimp in a   REGIONAL CLASSIC
mixture of coconut milk, tomatoes, cilantro and garlic, topped with beaten eggs and baked.

fritada de aratú a mixture of crabmeat, tomatoes, coconut milk and cilantro, covered with beaten eggs and baked.

fritada paulista codfish and potatoes cooked in coconut milk, covered with beaten eggs and baked.

fritas french fries.

frutas da época fresh fruits in season. Also called *frutas da estação*.   TRY THEM ALL!

frutas da estacão see *frutas da época*.

galeto na brasa charcoal-broiled chicken.   NATIONAL FAVORITE

galinha à cabidela a chicken stew with sauce made from the giblets and blood. Also called *galinha cabidela*.

galinha ao molho pardo a chicken stew with a brown sauce   REGIONAL CLASSIC
containing fresh chicken blood.

galinha cabidela see *galinha à cabidela*.

galinha com toucinho chicken with bacon.

galinha dessossada com recheio boned stuffed chicken.

galinhada com pequí chicken and rice flavored with *malagueta*   REGIONAL CLASSIC
peppers and *pequí* (souari, or butternut).

garoupa doré fried and breaded grouper fish, dipped in a mixture of mustard, ketchup and lemon.

garoupa escaldada com pirão boiled grouper fish with a mash of manioc meal moistened with the fish broth.

gelatina de côco coconut gelatin.

gemada de café coffee mixed with eggnog.

goiaba batida a frappé of guava paste, whipped egg white and *cachaça,* the Brazilian brandy made from sugar cane.

goiaba em calda guava fruit in thick syrup.

goiabada com queijo slices of guava paste and white cheese.

guarnição à francesa a mixture of peas, onions, thin strips of fried potatoes and ham.

guisado de carne com quiabo a meat stew with okra.

iscas de pirarucú ao molho tártaro an appetizer of *pirarucú* fish with tartar sauce.

jacúba a beverage of water, sugar or honey, and manioc meal.

joelho de moça (maiden's knee) a baked appetizer of bread dough filled with ham.

lagarta ao mostarda e champagne round steak baked in mustard and champagne.

lagarto recheado stuffed round steak.

lagosta com leite de côco lobster with coconut milk.

lagosta grelhada grilled lobster.

lagosta grelhada na brasa charcoal-broiled lobster.

lagostinha ao molho de queijo de búfala a small lobster in a sauce made from buffalo cheese.

lâminas de surubim defumado thinly sliced smoked *surubim* fish.

leitão assado com abacaxi roasted suckling pig with pineapple.

leitão pururuca roasted suckling pig basted with hot oil to make the skin crisp and bumpy.

leitão recheado roasted, stuffed suckling pig.

lentilha com paio lentils with pork sausage.

licor de mel a liqueur of vodka, honey, cloves, cinnamon and grated orange rind.

lingua com passas tongue with raisins.

lingua fresca com puré de batatas fresh beef tongue with mashed potatoes.

linguado frito fried sole.

lingüiça frita fried pork sausage, or pork and beef sausage.

lombinho tropeiro pork loin with beans and toasted manioc meal.

lombo assado pork loin roast. Also called *lombo de porco*.

lombo de pirarucú grelhado grilled loin of *pirarucú* fish.

lombo de porco see *lombo assado*.

lombo vacum beef sirloin steak.

lulas recheadas stuffed squid.

maçãs recheadas com passas baked apples stuffed with raisins.

macaxeira cozida stewed manioc tubers.

maçãzinhas candies shaped like little apples.

mae benta (mother benta) small cakes of coconut, rice flour and
eggs.

maionese de atum tuna salad with mayonnaise.

maionese de frango chicken salad with mayonnaise.

maminha assada fatiada sliced roast beef.

maminha de alcatra round steak.

maniçoba a stew of sun-dried meat, smoked pork loin, sausage,
calves and pigs' feet, giblets, smoked tongue, bacon and ground
leaves of the manioc plant *(maniva),* which give the dish its
characteristic dark green color.

manjar à brasileira a pudding of rice flour, sugar and milk,
browned in the oven and sprinkled with powdered sugar and
cinnamon.

manjar branco a pudding, or blancmange, made with cornstarch,
eggs and coconut milk.

manjar de côco com môlho de ameixas coconut blancmange with
prune sauce.

manjar de galinha a mixture of chicken cooked in milk, rice flour,
sugar and lemon rind, sprinkled with cinnamon.

mariscada (Brazilian bouillabaisse) large pieces of fish, clams,
mussels, shrimp and lobster in a tomato, saffron and cilantro
sauce.

mata nego (man killer) a drink consisting of coffee, black tea,
crushed anise, cognac, bitters and *cachaça,* the Brazilian brandy
made from sugar cane.

mate strong Brazilian cowboy *(gaúcho)* tea.

mate gelado iced mate tea.

maxixada a stew made with the small green *maxixi* squash,
tomatoes, shrimp and dried meat.

milho verde com queijo fresh corn kernels mixed with grated
cheese, cream and eggs.

mingau a porridge made from manioc meal.

NATIONAL FAVORITE **mingau de aveia** a porridge made from oats, topped with cinnamon or cloves.

mingau de maizena a porridge made from corn meal, topped with cinnamon or cloves.

miolo de alcatra a center cut of round steak, with the fat removed.

mixto quente a toasted ham and cheese sandwich.

moça doce (sweet girl) a baked sweet of manioc meal, ground peanuts, brown sugar and eggs, molded into loaves.

mocotó calves' feet and tripe simmered in claret, tomato paste and *malagueta* peppers.

NATIONAL FAVORITE **molho apimentado** a hot sauce made by combining some broth reserved from boiled black beans with *malagueta* peppers and with *molho campanha,* a sauce containing tomato, onion and green pepper in wine vinegar.

molho baiano a sauce made from a paste of *malagueta* peppers, smoked shrimp, fresh ginger and *dendê* palm oil.

molho brasileiro a sauce of *malagueta* peppers, cilantro, onion and lime juice.

molho campanha a sauce of tomatoes, onion and green bell pepper in olive oil and wine vinegar. This sauce also is called *molho vinagrete* as is a simpler dressing of olive oil, vinegar and seasonings.

REGIONAL CLASSIC **molho de acarajé** a paste of dried *malagueta* peppers, dried smoked shrimp, cilantro and ginger.

molho de azeite de dendê e vinagre a sauce of *dendê* palm oil and vinegar, seasoned with *malagueta* peppers, onion and cilantro.

molho de camarão miudo a sauce with tiny shrimp.

molho de pimenta e azeite de dendê a sauce of *malagueta* peppers in *dendê* palm oil.

molho de pimenta e limão a sauce of *malagueta* peppers and lemon juice, with onion and garlic.

DELICIOUS **molho de requeijão** a sauce made with a mild cheese resembling cream cheese or ricotta.

molho de tomate com amendoim a sauce of tomatoes, cream and ground roasted peanuts.

molho ferrugem a "rust-colored" sauce made from the juices of cooked meat.

molho inglês Worcestershire sauce.

molho nagô a sauce of puréed *malagueta* peppers, dried smoked shrimp, okra, or a small green squash called *jilo,* and lemon juice. (Many of the slaves in Brazil were members of the African tribe called Nagô.)

molho vinagrete a dressing of olive oil, vineger and seasonings. Also see *molho campanha*.

moqueca capixaba a stew from the state of Espírito Santo which is flavored with *urucu(m)* oil rather than *dendê* palm oil.   REGIONAL CLASSIC

moqueca de arraia a stew of stingray in coconut milk, tomatoes, onions, cilantro and *dendê* palm oil.

moqueca de camarão a stew of shrimp in coconut milk, tomatoes, onions, cilantro and *dendê* palm oil.   REGIONAL CLASSIC

moqueca de fato a stew of beef stomach.

moqueca de ovos a baked mixture of beaten eggs, dried shrimp, onion, garlic, and coconut milk, flavored with *dendê* palm oil.

moqueca de peixe a stew of fish filets marinated in lemon juice, garlic and tomato, then simmered in coconut milk, crushed coriander seeds and *dendê* palm oil.

mousse de castanhas de cajú e chocolate a cashew nut and chocolate mousse.   EXTRAORDINARY

mugunzá see *canjica*.

mugunzá de cortar a version of the hominy corn porridge called *mugunzá* that is thick enough to cut into pieces.

musse de açai a mousse made with the *açai* fruit.

nabo amanteigado turnips baked in a mixture of melted butter and bread crumbs.

ôlhos de sogra (mother-in-law's eyes) prunes stuffed with a mixture of egg yolk, sugar and coconut, and rolled in sugar.   NATIONAL FAVORITE

omeleta de camarão a shrimp omelet.

ostras de panela pan-fried oysters.

ovos cozidos boiled eggs.

ovos de codorna hard-boiled quail eggs.

ovos duros hard-boiled eggs.

ovos duros com molho do peixe hard-boiled eggs covered with fish sauce and toasted manioc meal, and served hot.

ovos escaldados poached eggs.

ovos estrelados com presunto fried eggs with smoked ham.

ovos fritos fried eggs.

ovos mexidos com trufas e queijo scrambled eggs with truffles and cheese.

ovos moles soft-boiled eggs.

TASTY **ovos queimados (burned eggs)** eggs cooked in sugar syrup until slightly browned, and flavored with cinnamon and cloves.

ovos recheados stuffed hard-boiled eggs.

paçoca a candy made of peanuts, sugar and manioc meal.

REGIONAL CLASSIC **paçoca de carne seca** a pulverized mixture of dried meat, bacon, onions and manioc meal, typically served with rice.

pãezinho a small bread roll.

pãezinho de batata doce a sweet potato roll.

pãezinho de maizena a cornstarch muffin.

SUPER **palitos de amêndoas** anise flavored cookies sprinkled with chopped almonds, cut into narrow strips and baked.

palmito frito fried palm heart.

NATIONAL FAVORITE **pamonhas (Brazilian sweet purses)** cornhusks stuffed with a thick paste of corn, sugar, spices, coconut, and manioc meal, and steamed.

pão de aipim bread made of sweet manioc flour and dried, grated white cheese.

pão de alho torrado garlic bread.

pão de centeio rye bread.

pão de ló sponge cake.

pão de milho corn bread.

NATIONAL FAVORITE **pão de queijo** a cheese roll.

pão rosca rusk.

VERY SWEET **papos de anjo (angel's cheeks)** small cakes soaked in syrup.

pastéis de carne meat turnovers.

NATIONAL FAVORITE **pastéizinhos** little turnovers.

pastel de galinha a chicken turnover.

patas de caranquejo crab claws.

patinho de carangueijo ao vinagrete marinated crab claws.

REGIONAL CLASSIC **pato ao tucupí** duck marinated in olive oil, lemon juice and garlic, and roasted. The meat is then boiled in *tucupí,* a seasoned sauce made with the juice extracted from manioc root.

pato com azeitonas braised duck with olives.

pato da fazenda ranch-style braised duck.

pavé de chocolate a rich dessert made of thin alternating layers of chocolate mousse and cake, or lady fingers. Also known as *torta de pavé*.

paxicá a stew made with turtle liver seasoned with lemon and pepper (turtle is an endangered species).

pé-de-moleque brasileiro (young boy's foot) Brazilian-style peanut brittle containing manioc meal and ginger. NATIONAL FAVORITE

peito de frango temperado com enchovas chicken breast seasoned with anchovies.

peixada baiana a fish stew with coconut milk and *dendê* palm oil.

peixada de mariscos a stew of fish, shrimp, mussels, and lobster cooked in onion, tomatoes, coconut milk, *dendê* palm oil and cilantro. REGIONAL CLASSIC

peixada pernambucana fish prepared in the style of the state of Pernambuco. Marinated fish filets are simmered and served surrounded by bundles of cooked vegetables.

peixe à brasileira Brazilian-style marinated, cooked fish with shrimp sauce.

peixe à carioca chunks of fresh codfish covered with a tomato-based shrimp sauce and garnished with hearts-of-palm. EXCELLENT CHOICE

peixe à escabeche marinated fish.

peixe amanteigado fish in drawn butter.

peixe com frutas carameladas fish grilled with caramelized fruits.

peixe com molho do mar fish simmered in a sauce of shrimp, clams and oysters.

peixe em molho de tangerina fish baked in a tangerine sauce.

peixe grelhado grilled fish.

peixe na chapa com purê grilled fish with mashed potatoes.

peixe na telha fish grilled and served on a tile. INTERESTING

peixe recheado baked fish stuffed with a variety of mixtures such as shrimp and bread crumbs.

pêras assadas a dessert of cored pears filled with condensed milk and raisins, lightly doused with sweet wine and baked.

perdiz com molho madeira partridge with Madeira sauce.

pernil de carneiro ensopado leg-of-mutton stew.

pernil de porco roasted fresh ham. NATIONAL FAVORITE

perú à brasileiro Brazilian-style stuffed and roasted turkey. NATIONAL FAVORITE

perú assado à california com fios de ovos roast turkey with fruit, garnished with fine strands of egg yolk cooked in syrup *(fios de ovos)*.

perú assado ao molho de cereja roast turkey with a cherry sauce.

REGIONAL CLASSIC · **pescada no tucupí** drumfish in *tucupí,* a seasoned sauce made with the juice extracted from manioc root.

petiscos candies made from grated hard cheese, sugar, egg yolks and lemon.

picadinho coarsely chopped meat, mixed with onions and tomatoes and seasoned with *malagueta* peppers.

picadinho à carioca a mixture of coarsely chopped beef, tomatoes, chunks of sweet manioc and plantains, seasoned with *malagueta* peppers.

picadinho de quiabo a mixture of sliced okra, diced beef, dried shrimp, tomato and onion. Also called *quiabada.*

SPICY · **picadinho de tambaquí** small pieces of *tambaquí* fish served with rice, an herb called *jambú* and toasted manioc meal.

picadinho do rio grande coarsely chopped meat with raisins and manioc meal browned in butter.

picanha com batata doce frita beef steak (rump) with fried sweet potatoes.

GREAT CHOICE · **picanha fatiada** beef steak (rump), sliced into strips.

pimentão recheado a stuffed green bell pepper.

pimentões sete de setembro (Independence Day peppers) sweet, green bell peppers filled with cooked carrots and peas and covered with sieved egg yolks.

pingado strong coffee with milk, served in demitasse.

pintado na telha pintado catfish grilled and served on a tile.

REMARKABLE · **pio nonos** spongecake spread with guava paste and powdered sugar.

pirão creamed manioc meal, tapioca, corn or rice flour.

pirão de arroz a molded porridge of rice flour.

pirão de leite a porridge of manioc meal and milk.

pirão de milho a molded mash of corn flour.

pirarucú à marajôara *pirarucú* fish in the style of Marajó Island.

REGIONAL CLASSIC · **pirarucú ao leite de côco** slices of *pirarucú* fish stewed in coconut milk.

pirarucú fresco na chapa grilled fresh (not salted) *pirarucú* fish.

pitú aferventados com molho tártaro boiled crayfish with tartar sauce.

pitú ao leite de côco crayfish in a coconut milk sauce.

pitú com cebolas e tomates crayfish boiled with tomatoes and onions, then removed from the shell and dipped in sauce.

pitú no espeto crayfish on a skewer.

polvo ao vinagrete octopus in vinaigrette sauce.

polvo graúdo whole boiled octopus.

ponche de framboesa raspberry punch.

porco recheado roast stuffed pork. WONDERFUL

posta de peixe à moda da casa a slice of fish, prepared in the manner of the "house."

posta de pirarucú seco ao leite de côco a slice of dried salted REGIONAL CLASSIC *pirarucú* fish in a coconut milk sauce.

prato de verão a summer fruit plate.

pudim de abóbora pumpkin pudding. DELICIOUS

pudim de bacalhau com ovos salted codfish with eggs.

pudim de claras com bacurí a pudding made with *bacurí* fruit in merengue shells.

pudim de claras de ovos a pudding made with egg whites.

pudim de galinha chicken pudding.

pudim de leite a sweet pudding of milk, condensed milk and RICH beaten eggs.

pudim de sardinhas a seasoned mixture of sardines, mashed potatoes and eggs, baked and served chilled.

purê de batatas mashed potatoes.

purê de macã applesauce.

queijadas a snack of grated coconut, sweetened condensed milk, INTERESTING grated cheese and egg yolks.

queijadinhas same as *queijadas* but smaller.

queijão a custard of eggs and sweetened condensed milk. REGIONAL CLASSIC

queijo assado chunks of firm cheese barbecued and served on a skewer.

queijo de coalho a cheese made from curdled, cooked whole milk, prepared as for *queijo assado*.

quentão a hot spiced drink of cloves, cinnamon, fresh ginger, lemon slices and *cachaça,* the Brazilian brandy made from sugar cane, traditionally served on St. John's day, June 24th.

quentão de vinho a mulled drink of red wine, orange juice and lemon slices, flavored with cloves, cinammon and fresh ginger.

quiabada see *picadinho de quiabo*.

quiabos com camarões e farinha okra and shrimp in a sauce thickened with manioc meal.

quiabos cozidos stewed okra with onions and tomatoes.

quibe cru an appetizer of Middle Eastern origin made with raw ground lamb or beef, bulghar wheat and onions.

quibebe cooked pumpkin with sun-dried meat.

quibebe de abóbora baiana pumpkin purée with dried beef, seasoned with parsley or basil.

quindão a rich, sweet upside-down dessert made with eggs and grated coconut.

NATIONAL FAVORITE   **quindim de yá-yá (young girl's dessert)** a smaller version of the dessert called *quindão,* made in a muffin pan rather than a round cake pan. (Note the plural of *quindim* is *quindins.*)

EXCELLENT   **rabada ensopada** oxtail stew.

rabanadas French toast covered with cinnamon and sugar.

recheio de castanhas e passas chestnut and raisin stuffing.

recheio de pão de milho corn bread stuffing.

repôlho com vinho cabbage with wine.

rim com cogumelos kidneys with mushrooms.

rim de vitela seasoned veal kidneys simmered in dry sherry.

TASTY   **risoles de camarão** turnovers with a shrimp stuffing.

risoles de milho turnovers with a corn stuffing.

risoto de mariscos rice with shellfish.

risoto de salsicha rice cooked with grated cheese and sausage.

rocambole de batatas a "jelly roll" made of mashed potatoes, eggs, milk and flour, and filled with various mixtures.

FLAVORFUL   **rocambole doce** a sweet jelly roll.

rodelas de tomate verde fritas sliced fried tomatoes.

rosbife roast beef.

rosca de maisena cornstarch rusk.

INTERESTING   **roupa velha (old clothes)** shredded flank steak in a tomato-based sauce.

salada de carne desfiada com cebolas e tomates a cold salad of shredded cooked meat, chopped tomatoes and onions dressed with oil and lemon juice.

salada de chuchu green squash salad.

salada de couve flor and agrião a cauliflower and watercress salad.

salada de frutas fruit salad.

salada de ovos e salsão egg salad with celery.

salada de palmito hearts-of-palm salad with vinaigrette dressing.   REFRESHING

salada de quiabo a salad of warm okra, often in a vinaigrette of onion, garlic and hot pepper.

salada de rabanete radish salad.

salada de repôlho cru coleslaw.

salada entreverada a mixed salad of lettuce and fresh vegetables served with vinaigrette. Also called *salada mista*.

salada gelatinada fruit or vegetable gelatin salad.

salada mista see *salada entreverada*.

salgadinhos de bacalhau an appetizer of minced salted codfish   SUPER mixed with mashed potatoes, eggs and seasonings, formed into balls and deep fried.

salmão com palmito salmon with hearts-of-palm.

salpicão de frango a salad with fried potatoes, chicken, and   REGIONAL CLASSIC olives.

salsicha frita fried sausage.

salteados na manteiga tidbits sautéed in butter.

sanduíche de lingua tongue sandwich.

santola recheada stuffed crab.

sarapatel a seasoned pork giblet stew.   REGIONAL CLASSIC

sardinhas grelhadas grilled sardines.

saudades (longings) sweets made of egg yolks, sugar and tapioca   HEAVENLY starch.

sequilhos baianos butter cookies.

sequilhos de côco coconut biscuits.

siri catado shelled crab meat cooked with tomatoes, garlic, onion, and coconut, and flavored with *dendê* palm oil.

siri mole com côco whole soft-shell crabs in a coconut-based sauce.

siri recheado empty crab shells stuffed with a mixture of minced   NATIONAL FAVORITE crabmeat, onions, tomatoes, cilantro and *malagueta* peppers, topped with grated cheese.

sonhos deep-fried fritters sprinkled with sugar and cinnamon.   SCRUMPTIOUS

sopa de ameixas plum soup, served over toasted bread.

sopa de amoras mulberry soup made with white wine, seasoned with sugar and cinnamon and served over toasted bread.

sopa de cabeça de peixe fish-head soup.

sopa de castanha do pará a creamy soup with ground Brazil nuts, tapioca flour and shrimp.

sopa de cebola gratinada onion soup.

sopa de côco a creamy soup of coconut, minced ham and chopped cashew nuts, seasoned with allspice.

NATIONAL FAVORITE **sopa de creme de palmito** a creamy hearts-of-palm soup.

sopa de feijão preto black bean soup.

sopa de grão-de-bico e lentilha chick pea and lentil soup.

sopa de hortelã mint soup with garlic, served over slices of bread and covered with a poached egg.

FLAVORFUL **sopa de mariscos** a seafood chowder containing scallops, shrimp, mussels, crab and coconut milk, seasoned with cilantro.

sopa de marmelos puréed quince soup with rice, lemon, sugar and cinnamon.

sopa de milho verde corn soup.

sopa de siri a creamy soup of crab seasoned with garlic and *malagueta* pepper.

sopa leão velloso a seafood chowder named after a Brazilian diplomat, with shrimp, clams, lobster and crab meat, and grouper fish seasoned with garlic, onion and coriander.

sorvete de abacate avocado ice cream.

sorvete de manga mango ice cream.

suco de abacaxi e beterraba pineapple and beet juice.

suco de goiaba guava juice.

suco de manga mango juice.

DELIGHTFUL **suco de maracujá** passion fruit juice.

supremo de frango ao creme de milho boned and breaded chicken breast with creamed corn.

sururú steamed clams.

suspiros (sighs) merengue with grated coconut.

SPICY **tacacá** a thin soup made of tapioca, dried shrimp, topped with *tucupí* sauce, a seasoned sauce based on the extracted juice of manioc root. Also called *tucupí tacacá*.

talharim com creme de leite buttered noodles with grated cheese and cream.

tambaquí na chapa grilled *tambaquí* fish. REGIONAL CLASSIC

tapioca com côco a thin fried pancake of tapioca and coconut. Also see *beijú*.

tapioca com queijo a thin fried pancake of tapioca topped with a slice of cheese and grated coconut.

tapioca cuscuz see *cuscuz de tapioca*.

tênder (pernil) temperado na brasa charcoal-broiled seasoned EXCELLENT CHOICE
pork leg.

torresmos fried pork fat and skin, or cracklings. NATIONAL FAVORITE

torta capixaba a seasoned torte or pie of fish, shellfish and REGIONAL CLASSIC
seafood mixed with palm hearts, covered with beaten eggs and baked. This traditional Easter dish from the state of Espírito Santo is eaten hot or cold.

torta de camarão maranhense a torte or pie from the northeastern state of Maranhão containing shrimp, potatoes, tomatoes, green pepper, flavored with dried shrimp, covered with beaten eggs and baked.

torta de carne de porco e abobrinha a savory pie with pork and squash.

torta de castanha do pará Brazil nut pie.

torta de cupuacú a layer cake with a pudding-like filling made IRRESISTIBLE
from the *cupuacú* fruit.

torta de legumes a vegetable torte or pie.

torta de pavé see *pavé de chocolate*.

toucinho do céu (heaven's bacon) a dessert of beaten egg whites and yolks added to a sugar syrup, and thickened with flour and ground almonds.

tripa de vaca à brasileira Brazilian-style tripe with vegetables.

trouxinhas de repôlho cabbage leaves stuffed with ground meat.

trutas com amêndoas trout with almonds.

tucunaré de forno baked *tucunaré* fish. REGIONAL CLASSIC

tucunaré frito com verduras fried *tucunaré* fish with vegetable greens.

tucupí tacacá see *tacacá*.

tutú à mineira cooked black beans mashed and mixed with manioc REGIONAL CLASSIC
meal. It is traditionally served with pork chops, *lingüiça* sausage and shredded kale.

unhas de caranguejo breaded crab claws.

vagens com alecrim e manjericão string beans flavored with rosemary and basil.

vagens refogado com carne moída sautéed seasoned beans with ground meat.

REGIONAL CLASSIC **vatapá** a thick yellow or yellow-orange purée of dried smoked shrimp, ground peanuts and cashews, bread crumbs, ginger, *malagueta* peppers, coconut milk, and *dendé* palm oil. It is also a stuffing for the bean fritter called *acarajé*.

vinha d'alho a marinade for meat, fish and seafood, consisting of lemon juice or vinegar, crushed garlic and seasonings.

REGIONAL CLASSIC **virado de feijão** black beans sautéed in olive oil, garlic, onion, kale, parsley and chives, puréed and thickened with manioc meal, traditionally accompanied by sausages, sun-dried beef, grilled porkchops and an egg. (Compare with *feijão tropeiro,* which has the same accompanying dishes, but the beans are whole, not mashed.)

vitamina de abacate a cold drink made of puréed avocado and milk.

vitelinha à jardineira small pieces of veal garnished with a variety of cooked vegetables.

xinxim de bofe stewed giblets.

REGIONAL CLASSIC **xinxim de galinha** a chicken stew with onion, garlic, ground peanuts and cashews, dried shrimp, ginger and *dendê* palm oil.

xuxu com camarão see *chuchu com camarão*.

Foods & Flavors Guide

This glossary is a comprehensive list of foods and cooking terminology in Portuguese, with English translations. The list will be useful in interpreting menus since it is impractical to cover all the flavors or combinations possible for certain dishes. Descriptions of the unfamiliar yet glorious tropical fruits are more detailed to make it easier to recognize them in the fruit stalls of the open-air markets and city sidewalks. Likewise, the characteristics of the indigenous fish are described for those who venture into the fishmarkets (a must) and then encounter them on menus.

à baiano/a in the Bahian style. Preparations typically contain coconut, *dendê* palm oil and *malagueta* peppers.

à brás a way of preparing saltcod, or *bacalhau,* with homestyle, fried shoestring potatoes and eggs.

à brasa grilled.

à brasileiro/a (or brasileiro/a) in the Brazilian style. This expression is widely used and broadly interpreted. One commonly encountered dish using this term is *arroz brasileiro* which is rice, or *arroz,* prepared the delicious Brazilian way. The rice is fried briefly in oil containing chopped onion, garlic, tomatoes and seasonings before being boiled, to ensure that the individual grains absorb the seasonings and are not sticky.

à california with fruit in syrup.

à campanha country style.

à carioca (or carioca) in the style of the *Cariocas,* the inhabitants of the city of Rio de Janeiro. This term is broadly interpreted. One popular dish is *picadinho à carioca,* a mixture of coarsely chopped beef with tomatoes, chunks of sweet manioc and plantains, seasoned with *malagueta* peppers.

à cavalo topped with a fried egg.

à delicia in a delicious manner. Another interpretation of the term is that mayonnaise is an ingredient in the preparation.

à dorê dredged in manioc meal and beaten egg and fried in butter until golden.

à escabeche marinated in a pickling sauce.

à florentina with spinach.

à gomes de sá a style of preparing saltcod, or *bacalhau,* with potatoes and black olives, and topping the dish with quartered hard-boiled eggs.

à grega garnished with small pieces of ham or bacon, carrots and raisins.

à jardineira garnished with a variety of cooked vegetables.

à milanesa coated with an egg and bread crumb mixture.

à mineira in the manner of Minas Gerais, a state in the southeastern region. Dishes typically have shredded kale, or *couve,* pork, and black beans, or *feijão preto.* The black beans often are mashed and mixed with manioc to become what is called *tutu.*

à moda da casa prepared according to the manner of the "house."

à passarinho in small pieces.

à paulista (or paulista) in the São Paulo style. There are many interpretations of this style. For some dishes, such as *camarões à paulista,* the preparation is predictable: marinated, unshelled shrimp are fried in olive oil and garlic.

à piamontesa garnished with a mound of rice and mushrooms.

à portuguesa in the Portuguese manner. This term is encountered frequently. It often refers to preparations of saltcod, or *bacalhau,* including one that has pieces of fish separated by alternating layers of tomatoes and potatoes.

à rossini with sliced mushrooms in thick gravy.

à sua escolha of your choice.

abacaxi pineapple.

abíu a light-yellow fruit up to 4 inches long, with a round to ovoid shape and smooth skin. Its sweet white pulp, surrounding 1 to 4 seeds, is eaten raw or used to flavor ice cream. Until completely ripe, the fruit contains a gummy latex.

abóbora pumpkin.

abobrinha squash.

abricó do pará the mammee apple. This large, nearly round fruit, weighing up to 2 pounds, has an orange-brown skin and orange pulp. It is eaten in the natural state or used to flavor ice cream.

abrideira apéritif or "opener." It is a local name for *cachaça,* the Brazilian brandy made from sugar cane.

abunã smoked turtle eggs (turtle is an endangered species).

acafrão saffron.

açaí a round, blue-black palm fruit about ¾ inch in diameter which tastes like black raspberries. The soft purple pulp surrounding a single round stone is made into a thick and somewhat gritty juice called "purple paste" by adding manioc meal and sugar. It is used to make wine and a flavoring for ice cream.

acebolado with onions.

acelga chard.

acém a cut of beef corresponding to our chuck or blade cut.

acerola the Barbados cherry. This round red fruit is about ¼ inch wide with three rather shallow longitudinal furrows, generating a trilobed appearance. The orange-colored and somewhat tart pulp is very juicy, rich in vitamin C and tastes like a sour cherry. It is eaten fresh or made into preserves and liqueurs.

açougue a butcher shop; also called *carniceria.*

açúcar sugar.

açúcar mascavo brown sugar.

açúcar queimado caramel.

aferventado/a boiled.

agrião watercress.

agridoce sweet–sour.

água water.

água de côco coconut water.

água mineral mineral water with (*com*) or without (*sem*) gas.

aguardente see *cachaça.*

agulha needlefish.

agulhão swordfish.

aipim the sweet variety of starchy manioc tuber. After the skin is removed, the tuber is cut into chunks, boiled or fried and eaten like potatoes. It is also called *mandioca doce,* meaning sweet manioc, and *macaxeira* (compare with *mandioca,* the bitter variety).

aipo celery; also called *salsão.*

alcachofra artichoke.

alcaparras capers.

alcaravia caraway.

alcatra one of several cuts of beef equivalent to round steak.

alecrim rosemary.

alface lettuce.

alfavaca basil.

alfenins sugary sweets often molded in the shapes of flowers, fish and animals and individually wrapped in paper.

alho garlic.

alho e óleo garlic and oil.

alho-porro leek.

almoço lunch.

aluá a fermented drink made with water and sweetened corn meal or rice flour. Another fermented beverage of the same name is made from pineapple rind.

Foods & Flavors Guide

ameixa plum.

ameixa-preta prune.

amêndoa almond.

amendoim peanut.

amora mulberry.

amora-preta blackberry.

angú a molded and salted corn porridge, similar to Italian polenta, which is served hot or cold. Sometimes the corn is replaced with manioc meal or tapioca.

ao ponto "medium rare" steak.

apertivo aperitif or appetizer.

apimentado/a peppery or spicy.

aracá a round to pear-shaped yellow fruit up to an inch long with light-yellow pulp becoming white at the center. Since the pulp is too acid to consume raw, it is used to make various confections, a flavoring for ice cream, liqueurs and a juice sweetened with sugar. Also called *aracá-do-campo*.

aracá-do-campo see *aracá*.

araticúm the mountain soursop. This almost round dark-green fruit is up to 6 inches in diameter and has a netlike surface with many short spines. Its juicy yellow pulp is somewhat sour, making it a less desirable fruit than the closely related *araticúm-do-mato*.

araticúm-do-mato the custard apple. It is a somewhat heart-shaped fruit that grows to 6 inches in length and has a smooth yellow-brown rind with red highlights. Its surface pattern is variable. Some fruits are covered with many flat, hexagonal facets; others have raised or embossed ones. The sweet granular pulp is creamy-white with a segmented center. It is used to flavor ice cream or enjoyed fresh. Also called *coraçao de boi* (bull's heart).

aratú marine land crab.

arenque herring.

argolinha a small biscuit or cookie.

arraia sting ray.

arroz rice.

aruá a type of mollusk.

aspargos asparagus.

assado roasted.

assado de forno oven roasted.

ata the sweetsop or sugar apple. It is a round to ovoid green fruit up to 4 inches long with many small bumps studding the surface. The segmented pulp is white, sweet and delicious, tasting somewhat like a pear. It is eaten fresh or made into a juice mixed with milk. Other names for *ata* are *fruta do conde* and *pinha*.

atum tuna.

aveia oats.

avelã hazelnut.

aves poultry.

azêdo sour; tart.

azeite oil. It usually implies olive oil, or *azeite de oliva*.

azeite de dendê a dense palm oil, rich in vitamin A, extracted from the nuts of an African palm acclimated in Brazil. It imparts a delicious taste, aroma and bright orange color to food. This oil is a classic ingredient of the Bahian cuisine of northeastern Brazil. Note, however, that it is high in saturated fat and should be sampled wisely and sparingly as with other tropical oils available at home.

azeite de oliva olive oil.

azeitona olive.

bacaba a small, purple-skinned palm fruit a little less than 1 inch in diameter. The somewhat oily, yellow-white pulp is eaten raw, made into juice, wine and syrups, or extracted to yield a clear yellow oil, which substitutes for olive oil.

bacabada a paste made from the juice of the *bacaba* fruit thickened with fermented manioc meal.

bacalhau dried and salted codfish.

bacuparí an ovoid orange-yellow fruit that grows to 2 inches long. Its sweet, translucent white pulp is eaten raw or made into sweets or jam.

bacurí a somewhat round, yellow fruit up to 5 inches wide. Its white, slightly tart pulp is made into marmalades, a flavoring for ice cream or is eaten fresh.

badejo a fish similar to the sea bass.

bagre the generic name for a large number of catfish.

banana banana.

banana ana a type of small banana also known as *banana nanica*.

banana branca a common variety of banana that is very similar to the *banana prata*. Both are about 6 inches long. Another name for this variety is *banana maçã*.

banana comprida a fruit similar to the plaintain but shorter. Also called *banana-da-terra*.

banana nanica see *banana ana*.

banana ouro a very small and thin-skinned sweet banana.

banana pacova(m) the plaintain. Individual fruits can be up to 12 inches long and typically are fried like potatoes.

banana prata the most common variety of banana; it has a thick skin and is about 6 inches long.

banana roxa a purple banana.

banana-da-terra see *banana comprida*.

bananada a solid confection made of bananas and sugar.

bananinha a little banana. It also means a small piece of banana paste (see *bananada*).

bandeja do dia the day's special; a set meal; worker's meal. Also called *prato comercial, prato do dia* and *prato feito*.

batata potato.

batata baroa a small tuber with bright yellow pulp, often used in soup. Also called *mandioquinha*.

batata doce a sweet potato.

batida a drink of fresh fruit juice and *cachaça,* the Brazilian brandy made from sugar cane.

baunilha vanilla.

bebida beverage; drink.

bebida não alcoólica a non-alcoholic drink.

bebida quente a hot beverage.

bem passado (bem assado) "well done" steaks.

berinjela (beringela) eggplant.

beterraba beet.

bife steak.

bife de lombinho porterhouse steak.

biribá a heart-shaped yellow fruit up to 6 inches long with bumps on the skin that darken with handling. The sweet white flesh is juicy and is enjoyed raw or made into wine. Also called *fruta condessa*.

biscoitos biscuits, cookies or crackers; also called *bolachas*.

bode goat; also called *cabra*.

bofe lungs or giblets.

boi beef.

bolachas see *biscoitos*.

bolas balls. It also means dips of ice cream for cones.

boldo chile a small plant used for making a tea-like beverage as well as for medicinal purposes.

bolinhos small cakes, cupcakes or balls.

bôlo cake.

bomba a silver straw used to drink the tea-like beverage called *chá mate* from a gourd called a *cuia*.

bombom a bonbon or sweet.

botequim a stand-up bar.

braço beef arm roast.

branco/a white.

broa corn bread.

brócolos broccoli.

bucho stomach.

búfalo buffalo.

bule pot; teapot.

buriti an ovoid palm fruit, about 2 to 3 inches long and covered with horny red-brown scales. The pulp, a thin orange layer between the rind and a large hard seed, is obtained by soaking the fruit in warm water to remove the rind. A juice is extracted from the pulp and mixed with sugar and manioc meal to make a beverage. The pulp is also made into a sweet paste called *saieta,* a fermented beverage called *chicha,* or is extracted to yield a red oil. Also called *miriti,* but the *miriti* is actually a different, but similar species.

butia an ovoid, yellow palm fruit about an inch long. It is eaten plain or made into a liqueur.

cabacinha do campo a pear-shaped yellow-brown fruit. The somewhat tart pulp is eaten fresh.

cabra goat; also called *bode.*

cabrito young goat (kid).

caça game.

cação shark.

caçarola casserole.

cacau the cocoa pod. This large ovoid fruit with prominent longitudinal ridges and a pointed tip is golden-yellow to dark-red and is up to 12 inches long. It grows directly from the tree trunk and the larger branches. The sweet white pulp is creamy and becomes a delicious juice, which does not taste like chocolate, the product of its seeds.

cachaça the Brazilian brandy made from sugar cane; also called *aguardente.* The term *pinga* is also used but can be derogatory and imply that the liquor is of a very green quality. In areas of the northeast, it is called *mel* (honey).

cachorro quente hot dog.

café coffee.

café completo a complete breakfast. This more elaborate Brazilian breakfast consists of coffee, a variety of breads and rolls, cake and some fruit.

Compare with the regular breakfast, or *café da manha*. In hotels, the breakfast included in the room rate can be lavish.

café da manhã breakfast. Brazilians do not make much of breakfast. This meal typically consists of coffee and some bread or rolls.

café fraco weak coffee.

cafezinho coffee with sugar served in demitasse.

caipira peasant (cooking).

caipirinha the national drink. It is a cocktail made from crushed lemon, sugar and *cachaça*, the Brazilian brandy made from sugar cane.

caititu wild hog (peccary). Also called *porco do mato*.

cajá the hog plum. It is an ovoid orange-yellow fruit 1 to 2 inches long. The yellow, somewhat acid pulp is a thin, very juicy layer surrounding a large central stone. It is eaten fresh or made into juice, jelly, wine and liqueurs, and a flavoring for ice cream. Also called *taperebá*.

cajá manga an ovoid orange-yellow fruit about 3 inches long. The flesh is juicy, pale and tastes like pineapple. It is eaten raw or stewed, and made into juice and a flavoring for ice cream. Also called *cajarana* and *taperebá-do-serta*.

cajarana see *cajá manga*.

cajú the cashew apple. This yellow or bright-red fruit is about 3 inches long and shaped like a bell pepper. It is actually a "pseudo fruit" formed from the swollen flower stem. The true fruit is the kidney-shaped cashew nut that grows at the tip of the cashew apple (see *castanha do cajú*). The yellow pulp is very juicy and somewhat acid. The fruit is enjoyed fresh or made into juice, wine, compotes, and a flavoring for ice cream. It has an interesting pear-like taste. (Note: the juice stains clothing indelibly.)

cajuada a sweet paste made from the pulp of the *cajú* fruit. It is also the name of a popular beverage made from its juice. The drink is also called *cajuina*.

cajuina see *cajuada*.

calabaça gourd.

calabresa sausage; also called *salsicha*.

calda syrup.

caldeirada a fish stew similar to bouillabaisse.

caldo broth.

caldo de cana the juice extracted from sugar cane; also called *garapa*.

camarão shrimp (plural *camarões*).

camarão seca dried shrimp. The large smoked variety is a necessary ingredient of Bahian cookery in the northeastern region.

camarãozinhos little shrimp.

camargo coffee with sugar and farm-fresh unpasteurized milk.

cambuci a yellow-green disk-shaped fruit about 2 inches in diameter. Its juicy pulp is eaten raw or made into jelly.

canela cinnamon.

capa spareribs.

capão capon.

caparari a large flat-headed catfish with dark "tiger-like" stripes and spots. It can be at least 4 feet long and weigh 40 pounds.

capim-limão lemon grass.

cará a purplish yam with brown skin.

cará do norte a type of yam.

caraguatá a small, almost round fruit with yellow skin. Its tart pulp is made into a juice.

carambola the star fruit. This oblong orange-yellow fruit grows to 6 inches long and has 5 or 6 longitudinal ridges. Crosswise slices are star-shaped. The crisp yellow flesh is eaten raw or made into preserves or pickles.

caranguejo mud crab.

carbonara a sauce for pasta usually made with ham and olives but sometimes featuring other ingredients.

caril curry.

carne meat.

carne branca white meat.

carne de boi beef.

carne de carneiro mutton.

carne de cordeiro lamb.

carne de fumeiro smoked meat.

carne de porco pork; also called *porco*.

carne de vaca beef.

carne de veado venison.

carne de vitela veal.

carne do sol salted, sun-dried meat. Also called *carne seca, charque* (sometimes spelled *xarque*) and *jabá*.

carne moida ground beef.

carne preta dark meat.

carne salprêsa salted meat.

carne seca see *carne do sol*.

carne verde fresh meat.

carneiro sheep (ram); mutton.

carniceria see *açougue*.

caseiro/a home-made.

castanha chestnut.

castanha do cajú the cashew nut. This nut grows at the tip of the "fruit" called *cajú*. It is enclosed in a green hull containing caustic compounds, which burn the mouth and lips if the nut is not roasted (see *cajú*).

castanha do pará the Brazil nut.

catupiri a soft cheese.

cavala mackerel.

cavaquinha a small lobster.

cebola onion.

cebolinha scallion. Also called *cebolinha verde,* or green scallion.

cebolinha branca shallot.

cebolinha capim chive.

cebolinha verde see *cebolinha*.

ceia supper.

cenoura carrot.

centeio rye.

cereais cereals.

cereja cherry.

cereja-do-rio-grande a sweet, ovoid cherry-like fruit about an inch long with an orange to dark-red skin. The green pulp, very juicy and slightly sour, is enjoyed fresh.

cerveja beer.

cerveja bem gelada well-chilled beer.

cervejaria a tavern specializing in beer; also called a *choparia*.

cevadinha barley.

chá tea.

chá-mate the strong *gaúcho* (cowboy) tea made from the leaves, or *mate*, of a shrub called *erva mate,* which grows in the southern region of Brazil. *Chá-mate* is drunk through a silver straw *(bomba)* from a hollow gourd *(cuia)*.

chaiote see *chuchu*.

champanha champagne.

charque see *carne do sol*.

charque de peixe salted and dried fish.

charque ponta de agulha sun-dried meat made from a cut of beef called *ponta de agulha* which approximately corresponds to our brisket or plate cut. In the markets, huge slabs of this dried meat can be found— simply marked "PA."

cheiros verdes a mixture of herbs.

cherimoya an oval to heart-shaped, green fruit, 4 to 8 inches long, with a variable surface pattern of either small bumps or indentations resembling thumbprints. The scrumptious white pulp is sweet and juicy and tastes like vanilla custard.

chicha a fermented beer-like beverage made from fruit or corn.

chicória chicory.

chimarrão sugarless *chá-mate* or *mate* tea.

chispe pig's foot.

choparia a tavern specializing in draft beer, or *chopp*.

chopp draft beer; blond pilsner.

chopp escuro light stout.

chopp preto dark beer.

chouriço Portuguese smoked pork sausage.

chouriço de sangue Portuguese blood sausage.

chuchu a pear-shaped light-green squash (sometimes spelled *xuxu*). Also called *chaiote*.

chucrute sauerkraut.

chuleta loin chop.

churrascaria a restaurant serving barbecued meats grilled on a spit.

churrasco a hearty carnivorous meal of many different barbecued meats grilled on a spit or on long skewers *(espetos)*. The meat is rubbed with coarse salt or brushed with a seasoned brine solution to keep it moist.

churrasqueto small pieces of barbecued meat on skewers, like kebabs.

cidra cider.

ciriguela an ovoid fruit about 2 to 3 inches long with a thin yellow-orange to red skin. The sweet yellow pulp is made into a variety of confections or eaten raw.

coberto/a covered.

coberturas toppings.

côco coconut.

côco amarelo a ripe yellow coconut.

côco de água soft, unripened coconut meat.

côco ralado grated coconut.

côco verde an unripe green coconut.

codorna quail.

coelho rabbit.

coentro fresh cilantro or coriander.

cogumelo mushroom.

colher spoon.

colher de café half a teaspoon.

colher de chá teaspoon.

colher de sopa tablespoon.

colorau the red seeds from the berry-like fruit of the annatto tree. The seeds, also called *urucu(m),* are coarsely ground and used as a condiment. The orange-red pulp covering the seeds is used as a food coloring.

com pele with skin.

comida food or cuisine. The food from each region and any city within a region will be designated "*comida . . .,*" meaning "cuisine typical of the specified area." For example, cuisine of the state of Rio Grande do Sul is called *comida gaúcha;* cuisine of Bahia is called *comida baiana,* cuisine of the city of Recife is called *comida recifense* and cuisine of the northeastern interior is called *comida do sertão,* etc. It is not practical to include a complete listing here.

comida típica typical Brazilian fare.

cominho cumin.

compota fruit in sugar syrup.

concha ladle; spoon.

confeitaria a candy shop or confectionary.

congelado/a frozen.

conhaque cognac.

contrafilé the sirloin portion of a T-bone steak.

copo a glass.

copo de água a glass of water.

coração heart.

coração de boi see *araticum-do-mato.*

coraçãozinhos chicken hearts.

cordeiro lamb.

cortado/a cut.

corvina croaker fish.

costela rib.

costela de boi beef rib steak.

costeleta chop or cutlet.

couve kale.

couve de bruxelas Brussels sprouts.

couve flor cauliflower.

couvert unordered appetizers, appearing on your bill unless you refuse them outright or leave them untouched. They can be a simple plate of olives or an elaborate tray of tidbits.

coxão duro one of several cuts of beef equivalent to (top) round steak.

coxão mole one of several cuts of beef equivalent to round steak.

coxas thighs.

coxinha an appetizer made of dough filled with chicken. Fillings other than chicken are specified.

cozido a stew with many different meats and vegetables.

cravo-da-india clove.

creme cream.

cruá a large cylindrical fruit reaching lengths of over 20 inches, with a yellow to purple rind. The yellow pulp is made into a drink.

cuca a cake made with yeast as the leavening agent.

cucura the Amazon tree-grape. This round purple-black fruit is up to 1½ inches in diameter and smells of wintergreen. The juicy white pulp, sweet to mildly tart, is eaten raw or made into wine. Also called *mapati* and *tararanga preta*.

cuia a bowl or container made from a gourd. It is traditionally used for the strong *gaúcho* tea called *cha-maté* and the soup called *tacacá* (see *Menu Guide*).

cupuaçu an oblong aromatic fruit closely related to the *cacau,* or cocoa pod. The large rusty-brown fruit, up to 10 inches long, has a hard woody case enclosing sweet light-yellow pulp. It is made into a delicious juice, jelly, puddings and liqueurs. The seeds are fermented to obtain a chocolate-like product.

cúrcuma turmeric.

cuscuz a dish made of steamed cornmeal.

da época in season (fruit, for example). A similar phrase with the same meaning is *da estação*.

da estação see *da época*.

damasco apricot.

de tudo um pouco small portions of different dishes.

defumado/a smoked.

dendê see *azeite de dendê*.

derretido/a melted.

descascado/a peeled or pared.

desfiado/a shredded.

desossado/a boned.

doces sweets.

doces caseiros home-made desserts.

dose serving.

dourada a large catfish with a gold or shiny-gray colored body and gold to orange-tinged fins, justifying its name, "the gilded one." *Dourada* can reach at least 4 feet in length and weigh 130 pounds.

dourado an orange-yellow fish resembling salmon. It is an important fresh-water game fish prized for its tasty flesh.

dura green (unripe) or hard.

durian an ovoid fruit, 6 to 12 inches long, with a thick yellow-green rind, covered with sharp and woody pyramidal spines. The cream-colored pulp resembles custard and, to some, it has an extremely unpleasant odor. It is eaten fresh, boiled with sugar, and used to flavor ice cream.

embalagem a doggy bag. There usually is a small charge for this service.

empada empanada. The dough, rich in butter and eggs, can be filled with a large assortment of mixtures. This savory pastry is typically baked.

empadão a family-size *empada*.

empadinha a bite-size *empada*.

enchova anchovy.

endro dill.

enguia eel.

enrolado/a rolled up.

ensopado a stew flavored with coconut milk.

entrada appetizer.

entrecosto (entrecôte) choice sirloin steak with the fat removed.

erva-doce anise.

ervas spices.

ervas aromáticas a mixture of herbs.

ervilhas peas.

escabeche marinade or pickling solution.

escaldado/a scalded.

escalfado/a poached.

especialidade da casa specialty of the house.

espeto skewer.

espinafre spinach.

espresso coffee without sugar.

espuma a frothy mixture of cooked fruit and beaten egg white.

estragão tarragon.
estufado/a stewed; braised.

faca knife.
farinha flour. Although a general term, it often implies manioc flour or meal.
farinha d'agua de mandioca coarse manioc meal.
farinha de mandioca lightly toasted manioc meal.
farinha de pão bread crumbs.
farinha de trigo wheat flour.
farinheira a container for serving manioc meal. It typically accompanies the salt and pepper shakers on the table.
farofa a mixture of lightly toasted manioc flour and melted butter resembling buttered bread crumbs. Various other ingredients typically are added.
fatia slice.
fatiado/a sliced.
fava broad bean.
fécula potato starch.
feijão bean.
feijão da colônia a small white bean.
feijão de corda red bean.
feijão fradinho a small beige bean with a black spot, resembling the black-eyed pea.
feijão manteiga wax or butter bean.
feijão mulatinho brown bean.
feijão preto black bean.
feijão soja soybean.
feijão verde green bean.
feito/a made.
fervido/a boiled.
fiambre cured cold meat such as ham. The term also refers to food suitable for travel.
fígado liver.
figo fig.
filé (or filet) steak.
filhó fritter.
filhote a catfish. This name is commonly given to the young of the giant catfish known as *piraíba*. Juvenile fish in the markets typically are about 3 feet long and weigh between 10 and 30 pounds.

flambado/a flamed.

folha de banana banana leaf.

fraldinha flank steak.

framboesa raspberry.

frango chicken.

frango de leite very young, tender chicken.

fresco/a fresh.

frigideira a mixture of ingredients (meat, fish or vegetables) topped with beaten eggs and baked (also see *fritada*).

frios cold cuts.

fritada the term for *frigideira* commonly used in the southern region of Brazil.

frito/a fried.

fruta fruit.

fruta condessa see *biribá*.

fruta do conde see *ata*.

fruta-pão breadfruit. The round to oval yellow fruit, 4 to 8 inches in diameter, has a surface with many small, 4- to 6-sided facets, often with short spines in the center. The fibrous yellow pulp, which tastes like a sweet potato, is eaten fried, baked or boiled, but not raw.

frutas em caldas fruit in syrup.

frutos do mar seafood.

fubá corn meal.

funcho fennel.

gado cattle.

galetaria a store selling chicken.

galeto barbecued chicken; also an informal restaurant specializing in barbecued chicken.

galinha chicken (hen).

ganso goose.

garapa see *caldo de cana*.

garfo fork.

garoupa grouper (fish).

gelado ice cream; better known as *sorvete*.

gelado/a frozen; iced.

gelatina gelatin.

gelatina em fôlha a thin sheet of gelatin used in making desserts.

geléia jelly; jam.

geléia de mocotó aspic made from calves' feet.

gema de ovo egg yolk.

gengibre ginger.

gergelim sesame.

goiaba guava.

goiabada guava paste.

goma tapioca powder.

gordura de côco coconut fat.

gorjeta a tip (gratuity).

grão-de-bico chick pea.

gratinado/a grated.

graviola the soursop. This large, asymmetrically heart-shaped, dark-green fruit is up to 12 inches long with skin bearing many soft short projections. The segmented white pulp is mildly acidic and has an aroma of pineapple. The sweeter fruits are eaten fresh. The pulp is made into juice, apéritifs and a flavoring for ice cream.

grelhado/a grilled or broiled.

groselha currant or gooseberry.

guaiamu(m) small land crabs.

guaraná the fruit of a woody climbing shrub. *Guaraná* is a fruit with a round orange-red capsule about 1 inch in diameter. When ripe, the capsule splits partially open, revealing a black seed covered with white flesh only on its innermost side, making it look astonishingly like a human eye. The edible portion, the seed with the white flesh removed, is rich in caffeine and is made into a popular, commercial carbonated drink of the same name. The seeds are also processed and sold in many of the markets. They are roasted, ground (see *guaraná em pó*), mixed with manioc meal and then allowed to harden, typically in short sticks. Small pieces are grated from the sticks and rehydrated with water to make a stimulating non-carbonated beverage.

guaraná em pó powdered *guaraná* seeds. This powder is mixed with sugar and water to make a beverage.

guardanapo napkin.

guarnição side dish.

guisado stew.

guisado/a stewed.

hortelã mint.

imbu the Brazilian plum. This yellow-green ovoid fruit, up to 1½ inches long, has a juicy white or greenish pulp, with the flavor of a sweet orange. It is eaten raw, or made into jelly and liqueurs. Also called *umbu*.

imbuzada a paste made by boiling milk, sugar and the juice of the *imbu* fruit until thick. This concoction is also known as *umbuzada*.

ingá a green fruit with a woody pod up to 12 inches long. The sweet white pulp is eaten raw. Also called *ingá-acu*.

ingá-acu see *ingá*.

inhame taro root yam.

intestinos intestines.

iogurte yogurt.

iscas appetizers.

jabá see *carne do sol*.

jabuticaba a round, purple-black berry-type fruit about 1 inch in diameter which grows all over the trunk and limbs of its tree. The juicy, white pulp is very sweet and jelly-like, and tastes like grapes. It is enjoyed fresh or made into juice, wine and jelly.

jaca the jack fruit. It is a very large, oblong fruit, reaching weights of over 100 pounds, with thick yellow-green skin studded with small hard projections. The fruit has little or no stem and grows straight out from the bark of the tree. The very sweet yellow pulp has a banana-like flavor, but unopened, the fruit has a disagreeable odor. It is eaten plain or made into compotes, jelly and a flavoring for ice cream.

jambo the rose-apple. The fruit is oval, about 2 to 3 inches long, with dark-red skin and rose scent. The juicy white pulp is somewhat spongy, with an apricot-like flavor. It is eaten fresh or made into preserves.

jambú an herb. The leaves and stem of the plant cause a very mild numbing sensation in the lips and tongue. It is a characteristic ingredient of *tucupí* sauce, a traditional product of the northern region of Brazil.

jantar dinner.

jaraquí a type of fish found in the Amazon.

jarra jar.

jarrête beef hock.

jaú a large olive-green catfish with the widest girth among this group of Amazon fish. This fish can be up to 5 feet long and weigh 220 pounds. It is not prized as a food fish in the Amazon, but is enjoyed in other regions of Brazil. Also called *pacumum*.

jenipapada a paste made from the pulp of the *jenipapo* fruit sweetened with sugar.

jenipapo an oval yellow-brown fruit, 3 to 6 inches long, with a short, hollow tube-like growth at its tip. Only edible when overripe, the brownish pulp has an unpleasant aroma but tastes like apples. It is eaten fresh or made into marmalades, liqueurs and a flavoring for ice cream.

jerimu(m) a variety of pumpkin.

jiló a small, green bitter vegetable, resembling an eggplant. It is also found in the markets labeled *jiló amargo,* meaning "bitter" *jilo.* Interestingly, it is an edible variety of deadly nightshade.

jinjibirra ginger beer.

kaki Chinese persimmon; also known by the Spanish *caquí.*

lagarto one of several cuts of beef equivalent to round steak.

lagosta lobster.

lagostinha small lobster.

lâminas slices.

lanche an afternoon snack (not lunch).

lanchonete an inexpensive, stand-up, fast-food café or snack bar. One usually pays first and then takes a ticket called a *ficha* to the counter to get the food.

laranja orange.

lascas another word for slices (see *lâminas*).

legumes vegetables.

leitão suckling pig.

leitaria a milk bar.

leite milk.

leite de côco coconut milk.

leite em pó powdered milk.

lentilha lentil.

licores liqueurs.

lima lime. This fruit in Brazil is pale yellow and often as large as an orange, resembling our lemon more than our lime.

limão lemon. The fruit is small, green and tart, having the qualities of our lime. When ordering a *caipirinha,* the national drink of Brazil, the traditional lemon component will be green!

língua tongue.

língua de vaca beef tongue. This is also the name of a type of leafy red spinach.

linguado flounder.

lingüíca Portuguese pork, or pork and beef sausage.

lombinho pork tenderloin.

lombo pork loin.

lote a small quantity or batch. Sometimes produce in the outdoor fruit and vegetable markets will be sold by quantity *(lote)* rather than by weight (kilogram).

louro bay leaf.

lula squid.

maçã apple.

macarrão macaroni.

macaxeira sweet variety of starchy manioc tuber; see *aipim.*

macia maminha very tender round steak.

maço bunch.

maçunim small mollusks.

maduro/a ripe.

maionese mayonnaise.

maisena cornstarch.

mal passado (mal assado) "rare" steak.

malagueta see *pimenta malagueta.*

malzibier a dark beer.

mamão a larger and less sweet variety of papaya.

maminha de alcatra one of several cuts of beef equivalent to round steak.

mandioca manioc, or cassava, a tuber rich in starch. *Mandioca* refers to the bitter variety, which is poisonous when raw. The hydrogen cyanide, or prussic acid, present in these tubers must be removed by extensive washing and cooking before the tubers become edible. Manioc meal, or flour, is made from the pulp after its juice has been extracted. Lightly toasted manioc meal is sprinkled over most foods or used as an ingredient in other dishes such as *farofa* and *pirão.* The juice extracted from the pulp is detoxified by boiling and it becomes the basis for *tucupí,* a traditional sauce of the northern region. Tapioca, the starch settling out of the extracted juice, is featured in many desserts and is processed into several types of flour.

mandioca doce sweet manioc; also called *aipim* and *macaxeira*.

mandioquinha see *batata baroa*.

manga mango.

manga-uva see *mangaba*.

mangaba a round to ovoid fruit, 1 to 2 inches long, with yellow skin, finely spotted or streaked with red. The sweet pulp is enjoyed raw or made into flavoring for ice cream. Also called *manga-uva*.

manguito a small mango.

maniva the leaves of the manioc plant, which are ground and used as an ingredient in some traditional dishes of the north such as *maniçoba,* a meat and giblet stew (see *Menu Guide*).

manjericão another name for basil (see *alfavaca*).

manjerona marjoram.

manteiga butter.

manteiga de garrafa clarified butter.

manteiga queimada browned butter.

mãos hocks.

mapati see *cucura*.

maracujá the passion fruit. The yellow, purple and red varieties are most common. This fruit has many small seeds surrounded by a delicious, juicy pulp, which is generally used for juice.

mari an oval, yellow-orange fruit, 2 to 3 inches long, with sweet, aromatic yellow pulp, which is eaten raw, sometimes mixed with manioc flour. Also called *umari*.

marimari a yellow bittersweet fruit in the form of a cylindrical pod about 15 inches long.

mariola a confection made of banana.

mariscada a shellfish stew similar to a bouillabaisse.

marisco shellfish.

marmelada a solid paste of the quince fruit.

marmelo quince.

marreco domesticated wild duck.

massa dough. It is also the generic term for dried pasta products.

mata-bicho (animal killer) another name for *cachaça,* the Brazilian brandy made from sugar cane.

mate see *chá-mate*.

maxixe a small bitter, squash-like, green vegetable with knobby skin.

medalhão a tenderloin steak.

médio "medium done" steak. Other terms for this are *meio passado* and *meio assado*.

meio passado (meio assado) see *médio*.

melaço molasses.

melancia watermelon.

melão melon.

mercado a market, often outdoors and in the center of town.

mercearia a small grocery store.

merluza a type of fish.

mexerica wild tangerine.

mexido/a scrambled (egg).

mexilhão mussel.

milhitos miniature ears of corn.

milho corn.

milho verde fresh corn.

miolo a center cut or portion of meat without fat.

miolos brains.

miriti see *burití*.

misto/a mixed.

miúdo/a tiny. In plural form, *miúdos* means giblets.

mixira preserves of fish in fish oil.

moela gizzard.

moído/a ground.

mole soft or ripe.

molhado/a moistened.

molho sauce.

molho tártaro tartar sauce.

molhos quentes hot (temperature) sauces.

moqueca a stew from the northeastern region of Brazil, flavored with *dendê* palm oil and coconut milk. It is traditionally prepared with fish or shellfish and cooked over high heat in a black clay casserole.

moranga winter squash.

morango strawberry.

moscada nutmeg.

mostarda mustard.

muqueca see *moqueca*.

murici the wild Amazon cherry. It is a berry-like yellow fruit about ¾ inch in diameter with sweet yellow pulp. It is eaten raw, made into juice, desserts, wine and a beer-like beverage called *chicha*. Also called *muruci*.

muruci see *murici*.

murupi a small, yellow wrinkled cherry pepper.

mussarela mozarella cheese.

musse mousse.

na brasa charcoal broiled.

na chapa meat or fish fried in its own juice on a flat grill.

na manteiga in melted butter.

nabo turnip; also called *rábano*.

nata cream.

nhoques a type of dumpling of Italian origin.

noisettes ball-shaped pieces made with a small scoop, e.g., melon balls. Also called *nozetes*.

nozes nuts.

nozete see *noisettes*.

óleo oil.

óleo de amendoa almond oil.

óleo de urucu(m) oil made from the berries of the annatto tree (see *colorau*). The oil is used as a substitute for *dendê* palm oil in the state of Espírito Santo.

omeleta omelet.

oregão oregano.

orelha ear.

ostra oyster.

ovelha sheep (ewe).

ovo egg.

pacú a silvery fruit-eating fish whose fins and flattened body have various amounts of orange coloration. This fish resembles the *piranha* but is larger.

pacumum see *jaú*.

padaria a bakery.

FOODS & FLAVORS GUIDE

paio pork sausage.

pajurá a brown fruit about 3 to 5 inches long with rough textured skin and an irregular ovoid shape. The sweet yellow-orange pulp is granular and somewhat oily. It is eaten raw.

palmito hearts of palm.

palmito amargo a bitter variety of hearts of palm from the *guariroba* palm, which requires cooking.

pamonharia a stand or shop selling *pamonha,* a paste of seasoned corn and coconut stuffed into a corn husk and steamed.

panqueca pancake.

pão bread.

pão amanhecido day-old bread; also called *pão dormido.*

pão árabe pita bread.

pão de centeio redondo a rye roll.

pão de forma sandwich bread.

pão dormido see *pão amanhecido.*

pão tostado toast.

pãozinho a small bread roll.

papaia papaya.

páprica paprika.

pargo porgy (fish).

parmesão parmesan cheese.

pastèizinho a bite-size filled turnover.

pastel a sweet or savory (meat or vegetable) turnover with pie-like dough. Note that the plural of *pastel* is *pastéis.*

pastelão a large family-size turnover.

pastelaria a shop selling pastries, especially the *pastel.*

patauá an oblong, deep-purple palm fruit measuring up to 1½ inches in length, which is rich in protein and oil. The pulp is mixed with sugar and manioc meal to make a juice, or is boiled to extract the light-green oil.

patinhas crab claws. Also called *patolas.*

patinho one of several cuts of meat equivalent to (top) round steak.

pato duck.

patolas see *patinhas.*

pavé a type of cake with several thin layers, each separated by a pudding-like mixture.

paxicá a stew made of turtle liver (from an endangered species).

pedações pieces.

peito breast.

peixada a fish stew.

peixe fish.

peixe espada swordfish.

peixe-boi manatee (an endangered species).

peixe-cachorro dogfish.

peneirado/a sieved.

pepino cucumber.

pequí the souari nut or butternut. It has a round to oval shape and green leathery skin. Both its granular pulp and seed kernels are eaten cooked, typically with rice or beans, or made into a liqueur. The seed case in some varieties has hard sharp spines, which must be very carefully removed.

pera pear.

perdiz partridge.

perna leg.

pernil leg. It primarily refers to pork. The meat is fresh, not smoked or cured.

perú turkey.

pés sujos (dirty feet) "greasy spoons," or bars, serving bar food.

pescada drumfish.

pescaria a shop selling fish.

pescoço neck.

pessegada a solid confection made of peaches.

pêssego peach.

petisco appetizer.

picadinho/a minced.

picado/a cut into small pieces.

picanha beef steak or roast from the rump. This popular cut has a characteristic layer of fat along one side.

picles pickles.

pilado/a pounded or peeled.

pimenta pepper.

pimenta malagueta a small hot, red pepper. It is a characteristic ingredient of Bahian cookery in the northeast.

pimenta-do-cheiro the very hot habanero pepper.

pimenta-do-reino black pepper (from peppercorns).

pimentão-doce bell pepper.

pinga see *aguardente*.

pinha see *ata*.

pinhões large pine nuts.

pintado a large striped catfish.

pipoca popcorn.

piracuí dried fish meal.

piraíba a giant gray catfish. It is both the largest catfish and the largest fish of the Amazon, attaining lengths of up to 10 feet and weights of 300 pounds. Juvenile fish are called *filhote*.

piranha a flat-bodied fish with notoriously sharp cutting teeth. The flesh is considered delicious but bony. Not all members of this group of fish are potentially dangerous; some are fruit and seed eaters.

pirão a mash made by adding broth or coconut milk to manioc meal, rice or corn flour and thickening it over heat. Traditional *pirão* is made with manioc meal moistened with broth reserved from boiled fish and is served with fish.

pirapitanga a large flat-bodied fish with blue-white coloration. It eats fruits and seeds, using molar-like teeth to crush them. This fish can weigh as much as 40 pounds and be 2½ feet long.

pirarara a large catfish with an oversized head. All of its fins are orange-tinged except for the tail fin, which is red. The dorsal surface is dark and mottled, in marked contrast to the white underside. It can be at least 4 feet long and weigh 100 pounds.

pirarucú a huge yellow-green fish. It is the largest scaly fish in Brazil, reaching lengths of at least 7 feet and weights of 275 pounds. This economically important fish is usually sold dried, requiring overnight soaking to remove the salt before cooking. The large (1 to 2 inches) brown-tipped scales have a rough surface that is useful as a fingernail file. The raspy tongue is dried and used as a grater.

pirulito lollipop.

pitanga the Surinam cherry. It is a red or dark-purple fruit about an inch in diameter with 7 or 8 longitudinal ridges on the surface. The mildly acidic orange-red pulp, surrounding 1 to 3 resinous seeds, is eaten fresh or made into juice, compotes, jelly, wine, liqueurs and a flavoring for ice cream. Excellent sauces are made with the sweetened seeded pulp.

pitomba a round fruit about an inch in diameter with yellow-green skin. The sweet-sour, translucent white pulp is eaten fresh.

pitú prawn.

pó powder.

pó aromático a mixture of cinnamon, nutmeg and cloves.

polpa pulp.

polvilho powder.

polvilho azêdo sour, finely ground tapioca starch.

polvilho doce sweet, finely ground tapioca starch.

polvo octopus.

ponche punch.

ponta de agulha a cut of beef corresponding to brisket.

porção portion.

porco pork; also called *carne de porco.*

porco do mato see *caititu.*

posta slice.

prato plate.

prato comercial see *bandeja do dia.*

prato do dia see *bandeja do dia.*

prato feito see *bandeja do dia.*

prato principal main course.

prato típico a typical Brazilian meal.

presunto smoked ham; also called *tênder.*

púcara a deep earthenware casserole.

pudim pudding.

pupunha the peach palm fruit. This ovoid fruit is about 1 to 2 inches long with yellow-red, orange, or even green skin when ripe. The yellow granular pulp, tasting somewhat like a sweet potato, is rich in vitamin A. It is boiled in salt water and eaten warm, often with honey placed in the depression left by the large seed. A fermented beverage called *chicha* is also made from it. In the markets, clusters of the fruit can be found still attached to the stems.

purê purée.

queijo cheese.

queijo de cabra cheese made from goat's milk.

queijo de minas a mild, white cheese, similar to muenster, which is made in the state of Minas Gerais.

queijo de sertão a dry cheese, often of goat's milk, made in the northeastern interior.

queijo do marajó buffalo milk cheese made on Marajó Island.

queijo prato a mild yellow cheese resembling American cheese.

queimado/a burned.

quente hot.

quiabo okra; also called *quingombô.*

quingombô see *quiabo*.

quitute tidbit.

rabada oxtail.

rabanete radish.

rábano another name for turnip (see *nabo*).

rabinho backside or buttocks.

rabo pig tail.

raizes roots.

ralado/a grated.

rapadura a hard, unrefined brown sugar eaten as candy.

rasgado/a shredded.

recheado/a stuffed.

recheio a stuffing for fish, fowl, *empadas* (empanadas), etc. and a mixture for canapés.

refeição meal.

refeição completa a special meal of the day, or *bandeja do dia,* that includes a beverage and dessert.

refeições caseiras home-made food.

refogado a preliminary step in cooking meat, fish or seafood, which involves lightly sautéeing it with onion, tomatoes, garlic and seasonings in a little cooking oil to seal in the succulent flavors.

refrêsco cool drink.

refrigerante soft drink.

repôlho cabbage.

repôlho roxo red cabbage.

requeijão a mild creamy cheese, similar to our cream cheese, made from curdled and cooked whole milk. It is also called *requeijão cremoso*.

requeijão cremoso see *requeijão*.

resfriado/a cold or chilled.

restaurante natural a vegetarian restaurant.

restos leftovers.

rim kidney.

risole a type of turnover with a crust coated with manioc meal. This covering is thicker and softer than that of the *pastel* turnover.

risoto a rice-based dish.

robalo a pike-like marine fish.

rocambole jelly roll cake.

rodelas slices.

rodizio the style of presenting hunks of barbecued meats on long skewers at tableside so diners can select for themselves what they want to have carved for their meal. This type of *churrasco,* or barbecue, is usually an "all you can eat" phenomenon and the food selections arrive at the table continuously.

romã pomegranate.

rosca rusk. Also a ring-shaped bread or cake.

rosmaninho another name for rosemary. Also called *alecrim.*

sabores flavors (of ice cream, for example).

sagú the name for both a wine and flour derived from the sago palm.

saieta a sweet made from the pulp of the *buriti* fruit.

sal salt.

sal grosso coarse salt.

salada salad.

salame salami.

salaminho pepperoni.

salgadinho (little salty) an appetizer; also called *salgado.*

salgado see *salgadinho.*

salgado/a salted.

salpicado/a sprinkled.

salsa parsley; also a tangy sauce or relish.

salsa picante chili sauce.

salsão another word for celery; also called *aipo.*

salsicha sausage; also called *calabresa.*

salvia sage.

sanduíche sandwich.

santola a variety of crab.

sapota a round or ovoid fruit, 3 to 6 inches long, with green-brown skin. The sweet yellow-orange pulp is eaten fresh or made into juice. Also called *sapota-do-solimões* and *sapota-do-peru.*

sapota-do-peru see *sapota.*

sapota-do-solimões see *sapota.*

sapotí the sapodilla. It is a brown fruit, 2 to 4 inches in diameter, with a rough surface and a very sweet, yellow-brown granular pulp that tastes like pears. From 3 to 12 seeds are placed radially at the center. The pulp is enjoyed fresh or made into jams and flavoring for ice cream. The sapodilla tree has a milky latex, or chicle, which was used in the manufacture of chewing gum. Fruits should be eaten when bordering on overripe so that the levels of latex and tannin are palatable.

sapucaia the monkey pot fruit. The mature fruit has a large, woody case, about 6 to 7 inches in diameter, enclosing hard seeds with edible kernels. The fruit becomes a trap for pesky monkeys whose hands get stuck in the case when they reach inside to get the seeds, one of their favorite foods.

sardinha sardine.

sem casca shelled.

sequilho biscuit.

serviço service charge.

siri sea crab.

sobre torradas served on toast.

sobremesa dessert.

solteiro one; single.

sopa soup.

sopão a minestrone-like soup.

só por encomenda made to order.

sorvete ice cream; also called *gelado*.

sorvete de casquinha ice cream cone.

sorvete quente hot ice cream.

sorveteria ice cream parlor.

sorvinha a round fruit up to an inch in diameter with dark-green skin and sweet pulp.

suco juice, usually fruit.

suflê souffle.

supermercado a large, modern, indoor food store; supermarket.

surubim a large, flat-headed catfish whose dark stripes are similar to those of the larger *caparari* catfish, but thinner and more vertical. This fish can be up to 3 feet long and weigh 20 pounds.

sururú a type of clam.

taça cup; also called *xícara*.

tainha mullet.

taioba the edible leaves from a variety of taro root.

talharim noodles.

tâmara date.

tamarindo the tamarind. The fruit has an irregularly curved, flat brown pod 3 to 6 inches long. The somewhat tart, red-brown pulp is thick and sticky and is eaten fresh, made into a beverage or used as a flavoring for ice cream.

tambaquí an economically important fruit- and seed-eating fish in the north that is equipped with powerful, molar-like teeth adapted for crushing its food. Its oval-shaped body has an olive-green back and a black underside. These colors meet unevenly at the midline, producing a pronounced jagged pattern. This fish, reaching lengths of 3 feet and weights of 60 pounds, is prized for its delicious flesh.

tamuatá a freshwater fish.

tangerina tangerine or mandarin orange.

taperebá see *cajá*.

taperebá-do-sertão see *cajá manga*.

tapioca the starch settling out of the extracted juice of bitter manioc pulp. When it is heated on a flat surface, the individual starch grains pop open and clump together into small round granules.

tararanga preta see *cucura*.

tareco wafer cookie.

tartaruga turtle (an endangered species).

taxa de serviço see *serviço*.

temperado/a seasoned.

têmpero condiment.

tênder smoked ham; also called *presunto*.

tereré cold *chá-mate* or *mate tea*.

tigela bowl.

tira gosto cocktail snack.

tomate tomato.

tomilho thyme.

toranja grapefruit.

torrada toast.

torrado/a toasted.

torta a turnover or pie. It can be sweet or savory.

tortão a large turnover or pie.

toucinho bacon.

tracajás a variety of turtle (endangered species).

trigo wheat.

trufa truffle.

truta trout.

tucumã a round palm fruit about 2 to 2½ inches wide with an orange or yellow-green skin. The yellow-orange pulp, which tastes somewhat like apricots, is rich in vitamin A and is eaten fresh or made into a wine called *vinho de tucumã.*

tucunaré a beautifully colored fish with a silvery body and a brown back. Behind the eye there is a characteristic mottled patch of black spots. It also has three vertical dark blotches along the midline and a black and yellow "eye" spot on the tail fin. *Tucunaré* is a prized food fish from the north.

tucupí a sauce, traditional to the northern region of Brazil, based on the juice extracted from the bitter type of manioc root.

tutano marrow.

uberabinha the black bean used in making *feijoada,* the national dish of Brazil (see *Menu Guide*).

um bocadinho mais a tiny bit more.

um dá pra dois one serving is enough for two.

umari see *mari.*

umbu see *imbu.*

umbuzada see *imbuzada.*

unidade one serving.

urucu(m) see *colorau.*

uva grape.

uxí an ovoid yellow-green, palm fruit, 2 to 3 inches long, with smooth skin. The granular, somewhat oily pulp is made into liqueurs, a sweet paste, a flavoring for ice cream and eaten fresh, sometimes mixed with manioc meal.

vaca cow.

vacum cattle.

vagens string beans (singular, *vagem*).

veado deer.

verde unripe, green or fresh.

verduras vegetables or greens.

vermelho red snapper.

vermute vermouth.

vieira scallop.

vinagre vinegar.

vinagreira red sorrel or roselle. It is a tropical shrub whose young leaves are eaten either raw or cooked. The fleshy, protective outer covering of the flower is used to make a sauce similar to cranberry sauce. The sesame-like seeds are used as a flavoring.

vinha d'alho a marinade of seasoned vinegar or lemon juice and crushed garlic for tenderizing and flavoring meat, fish and seafood.

vinho wine.

vinho branco white wine.

vinho de tucumã a wine made from the pulp of the *tucumã* palm fruit.

vinho espumante sparkling wine.

vinho tinto red wine.

vitamina a drink of juice mixed with milk.

vitela veal.

vôngole a type of shellfish.

xarque see *carne do sol*.

xerém coarsely ground corn.

xícara see *taça*.

ximxim stew.

xuxu see *chuchu*.

zamboa a type of cider.

zimbro juniper.

Bibliography

Balick, Michael J. Useful plants of Amazonia: a resource of global importance. In *Amazonia: Key Environments*, edited by Ghillean T. Prance and Thomas E. Lovejoy, pp. 339–368. Oxford, England: Pergamon Press Ltd, 1985.

Barbosa, Glorinha. *Arroz, Feijão E . . . .* Uberaba, Minas Gerais, Brazil: Creche Comunitária Vovó Adelina, 1992.

Bastide, Roger. *The African Religions of Brazil: Toward a Sociology of the Interpenetration of Civilizations.* Baltimore, MD: The Johns Hopkins University Press, 1978.

Batchelor, Courtenay M. *Stories and Storytellers of Brazil, Volume I: Folklore.* Cuba: La Habana, 1953.

Botafogo, Dolores. *The Art of Brazilian Cookery.* New York: Hippocrene Books, 1993.

Boxer, Charles R. *Four Centuries of Portuguese Expansion, 1415–1825: A Succinct Survey.* Johannesburg, South Africa: Witwatersrand University Press, 1965.

Boxer, Charles R. *Portuguese Society in the Tropics: The Municipal Councils of Goa, Macao, Bahia, and Luanda, 1510–1800.* Madison, WI: The University of Wisconsin Press, 1965.

Boxer, Charles R. *Race Relations in the Portuguese Colonial Empire, 1415–1825.* Oxford, England: Clarendon Press, 1963.

Bradbury, Alex. *Backcountry Brazil: The Pantanal, Amazon and North-east Coast.* Bucks, England: Bradt Publications, 1990.

Brown, Cora, Rose Brown and Bob Brown. *The South American Cook Book Including Central America, Mexico and the West Indies.* New York: Doubleday, Doran & Co., Inc., 1943.

Cavalcante, Paulo B. Edible palm fruits of the Brazilian Amazon. *Principes* (USA) 21(3):91–102, 1977.

Cavalcante, Paulo B. *Frutas Comestíveis da Amazônia*, 5th edition. Belém, Amazonas, Brazil: Museu Paraense Emílio Goeldi, 1991.

Cleary, David, Dilwyn Jenkins, Oliver Marshall and Jim Hine. *The Real Guide: Brazil.* New York: Prentice Hall, 1990.

Dahlgren, B. E. *Tropical and Subtropical Fruits.* Chicago, IL: Chicago Natural History Museum Press, 1947.

Davidson, Alan and Charlotte Knox. *Fruit: A Connoisseur's Guide and Cookbook.* New York: Simon and Schuster, 1991.

de Andrade, Hermelinda Lys Carneiro. *A Cozinha Baiana: no Restaurante Senac do Pelourinho.* Salvador, Bahia, Brazil: Senac, Departamento Regional na Bahia, 1992.

de Andrade, Margarette. *Brazilian Cookery: Traditional and Modern*, 5th edition. Rio de Janeiro, Brazil: A Casa do Livro Eldorado, 1985.

Denslow, Julie S. and C. Padoch, editors. *People of the Tropical Rain Forest.* Berkeley, CA: University of California Press, 1988.

DeWitt, Dave and Paul W. Bosland. *The Pepper Garden: From the Sweetest Bell to the Hottest Habanero.* Berkeley, CA: Ten Speed Press, 1993.

dos Reis, José A. *Salvador: History and Images.* Salvador, Bahia, Brazil: Projeto Abraxas, 1987.

Draffen, Andrew, Robert Strauss and Deanna Swaney. *Brazil: A Travel Survival Kit.* Victoria, Australia: Lonely Planet Publications, 1992.

Freyre, Gilberto. *The Masters and the Slaves: A Study in the Development of Brazilian Civilization.* Berkeley, CA: University of California Press, 1986.

Goulding, Michael. Ecology and management of migratory food fishes of the Amazon basin. In *Tropical Rainforests: Diversity and Conservation*, edited by Frank Almeda and Catherine M. Pringle, pp. 71–83. San Francisco, CA: California Academia of Sciences and Pacific Division, American Association for the Advancement of Science, 1988.

Goulding, Michael. *The Fishes and the Forest: Explorations in Amazonian Natural History.* Berkeley, CA: University of California Press, 1980.

Goulding, Michael. Forest fishes of the Amazon. In *Amazonia: Key Environments*, edited by Ghillean T. Prance and Thomas E. Lovejoy, pp. 267–276. Oxford, England: Pergamon Press Ltd, 1985.

Guenther, Konrad. *A Naturalist in Brazil.* New York: Houghton Mifflin Co., 1931.

Harris, Jessica B. *Tasting Brazil: Regional Recipes and Reminiscences.* New York: Macmillan Publishing Company, 1992.

Leonard, Jonathan N. *Foods of the World Recipes: Latin American Cooking.* New York: Time–Life Books, 1968.

Leonard, Jonathan N. *Latin American Cooking.* New York: Time–Life Books, 1968.

Leroux, Guy. *Brazilian Cooking.* Singapore: Les Éditions du Pacifique, 1987.

Menninger, Edwin A. *Edible Nuts of the World.* Stuart, FL: Horticulture Books, Inc., 1977.

Morrison, Tony, editor. *Margaret Mee: In Search of Flowers of the Amazon Forests: Diaries of an English Artist Reveal the Beauty of the Vanishing Rainforest.* Woodbridge, Suffolk, England: Nonesuch Expeditions, 1988.

Morton, Julia F. *Fruits of Warm Climates.* Miami, FL: Julia F. Morton, 1987.

Nagy, Steven and Philip E. Shaw. *Tropical and Subtropical Fruits: Composition, Properties and Uses.* Westport, CT: AVI Publishing, Inc., 1980.

Nagy, Steven, Philip E. Shaw and Wilfred F. Wardowski, editors. *Fruits of Tropical and Subtropical Origin: Composition, Properties and Uses.* Florida: Florida Science Source, Inc., 1990.

Ortiz, Elisabeth L. *The Book of Latin American Cooking.* New York: Vintage Books, 1979.

Popenoe, Wilson. *Manual of Tropical and Subtropical Fruits.* New York: Hafner Press, 1920.

Purseglove, J. W. *Tropical Crops: Dicotyledons.* London, England: Longman Group UK Ltd, 1968.

Rehm, Sigmund and Gustav Espig. *The Cultivated Plants of the Tropics and Subtropics: Cultivation, Economic Value, Utilization.* Stuttgart, West Germany: Verlag Josef Margraf, 1991.

Rojas-Lombardi, Felipe. *The Art of South American Cooking.* New York: Harper Collins Publishers, 1991.

Samson, Jules A. *Tropical Fruits*, 2nd edition. Essex, England: Longman Group UK Ltd, 1986.

Schurz, William Lytle. *Brazil: The Infinite Country.* New York: E.P. Dutton & Co., Inc., 1961.

Shoumatoff, Alex. *The Rivers Amazon.* San Francisco, CA: Sierra Club Books, 1978.

Smith, Nigel J.H. *Man, Fishes, and the Amazon.* New York: Columbia University Press, 1981.

Smith, Nigel J.H., J.T. Williams, Donald L. Plucknett and Jennifer P. Talbot. *Tropical Forests and Their Crops.* Ithaca, New York: Comstock Publishing Associates, 1992.

Tume, Lynelle. *Latin American Cookbook.* Australia: Paul Hamlyn Pty Ltd, 1979.

Uhl, Michael. *Frommer's Comprehensive Travel Guide: Brazil '91–'92.* New York: Prentice Hall Press, 1991.

Wagley, Charles. *An Introduction to Brazil.* New York: Columbia University Press, 1971.

Index

⚅ Have a Perfect Trip.
Take along an EAT SMART guide, and dine with confidence!

Praise for the EAT SMART series:

Eat Smart in Mexico *offers what is most important about Mexican food and culture wrapped in a nutshell. If you cannot get to Mexico, this book will provide vicarious travel and cooking inspiration of the first order.*
> —Maricel Presilla, Ph.D., culinary historian and author specializing in the cuisines of Latin America and Spain

[**Eat Smart in Brazil**] *adds ¡Ole! to the kitchen.*
> —Florence Fabricant, New York Times

Soundly researched, clearly written, artistically illustrated, **Eat Smart in Indonesia** *is the most comprehensive and readable survey of the whole scope of Indonesian gastronomy I have ever come across. It is equally valuable as a solid reference work for the scholar and as exotic inspiration for the chef or home entertainer.*
> —Bill Dalton, Founder, Moon Travel Guides,
> Author, *Indonesian Handbook*

Well researched, accurate and very informative.
> —Chile Pepper magazine

Good reference for the kitchen or to take on a visit.
> —Chicago Tribune

The authors thoroughly educate your palate— eliminating any guesswork that could muddy the chances of a mouth-watering experience.
> —Bloomsbury Review

ORDER FORM

Use this form to order additional copies of **Eat Smart in Brazil: How to Decipher the Menu, Know the Market Foods and Embark on a Tasting Adventure**, or to order any of the other fine guidebooks in the **EAT SMART** series.

Please send me:

_____ copies of **Eat Smart in Brazil (2nd Edition)** - $13.95

_____ copies of **Eat Smart in Peru** - $13.95

_____ copies of **Eat Smart in Turkey (2nd Edition)** - $13.95

_____ copies of **Eat Smart in India** - $13.95

_____ copies of **Eat Smart in Indonesia** - $12.95

_____ copies of **Eat Smart in Mexico** - $12.95

_____ copies of **Eat Smart in Morocco** - $12.95

_____ copies of **Eat Smart in Poland** - $12.95

Add $2.50 postage for one book, $1.00 for each additional book. Wisconsin residents add 5% sales tax. For international orders, please inquire about postal charges.

Check enclosed for $ _____

Please charge my: VISA_____   MASTERCARD_____

Card # _____ Exp. _____

Signature: _____

Name: _____

Address: _____

City: _____ State: _____ Zip: _____

Telephone: _____

Email: _____

Mail this form to:

GINKGO PRESS
P.O. Box 5346
Madison, Wisconsin 53705

Tel: 888-280-7060 • Fax: 608-233-0053
www.ginkgopress.com • info@ginkgopress.com

NOTES

design   Ekeby
cover design   Susan P. Chwae
color printing   Batson Printing, Inc.
text printing and binding   Batson Printing, Inc.

typefaces   Garamond Simoncini and Helvetica Black
paper   60# White